**W9-AKD-956**

Zim, Herbert S.
Reptiles and amphibians

**DATE DUE**        $4.95

| | | |
|---|---|---|
| JA 2'90 | JUN 21 96 | |
| MY 14 90 | MAY 27 '97 | |
| MR 29'91 | OCT 15 98 | |
| SE 20'91 | MY 29 01 | |
| JE 22'92 | SE 15 01 | |
| JY 17'92 | OC 31 02 | |
| SE 11'92 | JE 10 04 | |
| NO 3'92 | DE 20 04 | |
| FE 27'93 | AG 05 05 | |
| JY 24'93 | OC 04 06 | |
| NOV 30 95 | SE 12 17 | |
| FEB 1 5 98 | SE 25 19 | |

# 212 SPECIES IN FULL COLOR

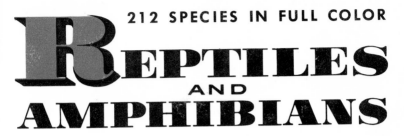

# REPTILES
## AND
# AMPHIBIANS

*A GUIDE TO FAMILIAR AMERICAN SPECIES*

by
## HERBERT S. ZIM, Ph.D.
and
## HOBART M. SMITH, Ph.D.
Department of Zoology, University of Illinois, and
Formerly President, Herpetologists League

## ILLUSTRATED BY JAMES GORDON IRVING

Sponsored by The Wildlife Management Institute

*A GOLDEN NATURE GUIDE*

## GOLDEN PRESS • NEW YORK

# FOREWORD

So many people of all ages want to know about snakes and turtles, frogs and salamanders, that the Golden Nature Guides would be incomplete without an introduction to reptiles and amphibians.

The authors express their grateful thanks to all who helped in making the book. Thanks are due to Charles M. Bogert and Bessie M. Hecht, of the American Museum of Natural History; James A. Oliver, of the N. Y. Zoological Society; Carl F. Kauffeld, of the Staten Island Zoological Society; Roger and Isabelle Conant, of the Philadelphia Zoological Garden; Robert C. Miller, Joseph R. Slevin, and Earl S. Herald, of the California Academy of Sciences; L. M. Klauber, C. B. Perkins, and C. S. Shaw of the Zoological Society of San Diego; Louis W. Ramsey, of Texas Christian University; and William H. Stickel, of the Patuxent Research Refuge.

Special thanks are due to our colleagues at the University of Illinois—Philip and Dorothy Smith, Harold Kerster, Donald Hoffmeister, and many others. Our gratitude goes also to James Gordon Irving for his fine cooperation and to Grace Crowe Irving; to Rozella Smith and Sonia Bleeker Zim for their assistance; and finally to our publishers for their untiring aid.

In the present revision, five additional pages of information have been added, plus a listing of scientific names. We hope readers will find this fuller and more attractive volume more useful.

H. S. Z.
H. M. S.

# USING THIS BOOK

The first step in the use of this book is to learn the differences between reptiles and amphibians:

## REPTILES

Usually: four-legged (except snakes and a few lizards); each foot with three to five clawed toes; skin usually with horny scales, sometimes bony plates. Most lay eggs with hard or leathery skin.

**1. TURTLES**   Leathery or bony shell. Four limbs, short tail. Head can be withdrawn wholly or partly into shell.   **pages 18-43**

**2. LIZARDS**   In the United States, mostly small, four-legged, covered with equal-sized horny, smooth or beaded scales. Most are egg-laying, fast-moving land reptiles. **pages 44-69**

**3. SNAKES**   Long, legless. Scales on belly usually larger than others. Jaws loose, mouth large. Lack ear openings. Some are egg-laying; some live-bearing.   **pages 70-113**

**4. ALLIGATORS and CROCODILES** Large, lizard-like. Skull forming long snout. Adapted to water life in warm regions.   **pages 114–115**

## AMPHIBIANS

Four- or, rarely, two-legged (except tadpoles). Smooth or warty skin, usually moist. No visible scales. Toes never clawed. Eggs usually in jelly-like masses in water.

**1. FROGS and TOADS**   Adults with larger hind limbs; tadpoles limbless when young. Adults lack tail. Most lay jelly-like eggs in water.
   **pages 118-136**

**2. SALAMANDERS**   Most have four limbs, even the larvae. Limbs about same size. Adults have tails.   **pages 137-153**

The introduction to each section in the book gives more details. Use illustrations for further identification. Pages 8-14 explain range maps and suggest activities. Index is on pages 158-160, scientific names on 155-157.

**TURTLE**

**LIZARD**

**SNAKE**

**ALLIGATOR**

**FROG**

**SALAMANDER**

3

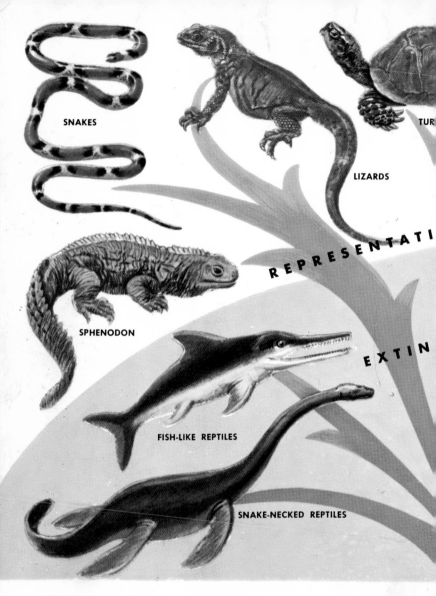

SNAKES

LIZARDS

TUR

SPHENODON

REPRESENTATI

EXTIN

FISH-LIKE REPTILES

SNAKE-NECKED REPTILES

**REPTILES** have a history which begins nearly 250 million years ago. The group slowly spread, and finally took over the land. Dinosaurs included the largest land animals. Other reptiles took to the air and to the seas.

CROCODILIANS

BIRDS

TOOTHED BIRDS

VING FORMS

ORMS

DINOSAURS

FLYING REPTILES

MAMMALS

MAMMAL-LIKE REPTILES

Some were swift, some were armored, some were terrible killers. As the climate changed, nearly all the great reptiles died off. Reptiles of today are interesting descendants of magnificent ancestors.

**SPADEFOOTS**

**TOADS and kin**

**SLIMY SALAMANDER and kin**

**FIRE-BELLIED TOADS and kin**

**TRUE AND NARROW-MOUTHED FROGS**

**REPRESENTATIVE LIVING FORMS**

**TAILED TOADS**

**EXTIN**

**ERYOPS**

**REPTILES**

**SEYMOURIA**

**AMPHIBIANS** had at least a 50-million-year head start on reptiles, but these first land animals never became completely independent of water. Their jelly-like eggs could not survive in air, so amphibians had to return to

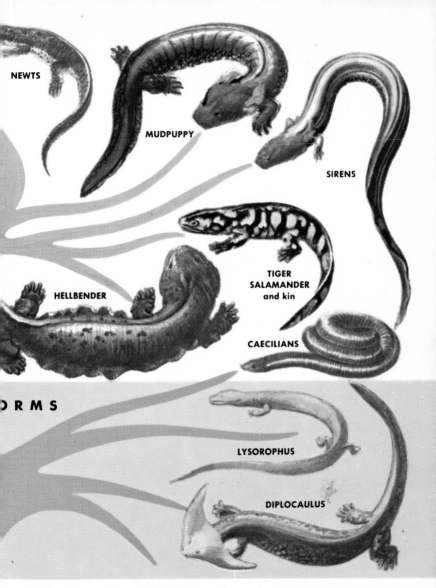

NEWTS

MUDPUPPY

SIRENS

TIGER
SALAMANDER
and kin

HELLBENDER

CAECILIANS

ORMS

LYSOROPHUS

DIPLOCAULUS

swamps, ponds, or streams to breed. Ancestors of present-day frogs and salamanders flourished in the Coal Age swamps. Many were clumsy giants. For more about living American amphibians, see pp. 116-153.

# SEEING AND STUDYING
# REPTILES AND AMPHIBIANS

**DESERT IGUANA**

**COMMON TOAD**

Maps in this book show approximate ranges of our familiar species. Where a map shows ranges of more than one species, the name of each species is placed within or next to the color or kind of hatching that shows its range. Overlapping of color and hatch indicates overlapping of ranges.

**FACT AND FABLE** This book brings together interesting facts and reliable scientific opinions. Sometimes the facts are stranger than fables; sometimes fables you hear are exaggerations or distortions of a small truth. Because some people have mistaken ideas about reptiles and amphibians, they destroy harmless species. We need not fear what we understand; so try to understand these animals.

**INTEREST AND CURIOSITY** While some people fear reptiles, most want to see what snakes, lizards, turtles, and frogs are really like. This curiosity has been fed partly by the fables about these creatures and partly by their unusual appearance. Every group of

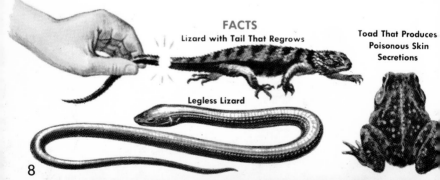

FACTS
Lizard with Tail That Regrows

Toad That Produces
Poisonous Skin
Secretions

Legless Lizard

8

animals includes strange and unusual kinds and, as a group, reptiles and amphibians have the richest share. Reptiles and amphibians have iridescent skin and varied patterns of color that few other animals can equal. They are attractive as well as interesting.

**VALUES OF REPTILES**   Reptiles were in their heyday millions of years ago; now they are only a remnant of a once-great group. Some are of direct value. We use the skins of alligators, lizards, and large snakes for leather. Turtle meat is a delicacy, as is the meat of larger lizards. Turtle eggs are eaten, and turtle shell has been used to make combs and ornaments. Even the venom of poisonous snakes has uses in medicine. In North America, the poisonous snakes are the only reptiles considered very dangerous. But the deaths from snakebite average only 150 per year. Reptiles feed partly on rats, mice, gophers, insects, and other pests; in turn they are eaten by mammals and large birds. As a group they are neither "good" nor "bad," but are interesting and unusual, although of minor importance. If they should all disappear, it would not make much difference one way or the other.

**VALUES OF AMPHIBIANS**   In evolution, amphibians were the ancestors of the reptiles. To us they are

FABLES

Snake
Rolling Like
Hoop

Bird Hypnotized
by Snake

Toad
Causing
Warts

9

less conspicuous and probably less important. Frogs and other amphibians are used in scientific experiments. We eat frogs' legs, and frogs consume quantities of insects. Here the usefulness ends. Yet, like the reptiles, these animals are part and parcel of  the animal world. They are curious reminders of animal life of long ago.

**CONSERVATION**   Most kinds of reptiles and amphibians should be protected, for our own enjoyment and for the future. Needless killing, so often based on fear and misunderstanding, should stop. No reptiles  should be killed, except poisonous snakes near human habitations. Perhaps even more important is the preservation of wild areas where reptiles, amphibians, and other wild life live. The cutting of forests, draining of swamps, damming of rivers, and even building of roads in wilderness areas all have a long-range effect on plant and animal life. The preservation of unspoiled land in state and national parks and forests, the wildlife refuges, the wilderness areas, and the like is important in the conservation program. And the swamps and marshes on farmland are worth keeping too.

Many reptiles die as an indirect result of their being cold-blooded. Snakes often come out on roads at night, possibly because of the warmth of the pavement. Turtles are constantly crossing highways, too. An early morning ride will show the toll taken by passing cars—a toll that could be reduced by more care on the part of motorists.

**LEARN TO KNOW THEM**   Learn to know reptiles and amphibians from books and, better, from life. Learn those in your region first. Be able to recognize poisonous snakes at a glance. Besides the zoo, make use of museums and exhibits. Become familiar enough with lizards, turtles, snakes, frogs, and salamanders to recognize common ones seen in the field.

**FIELD STUDIES** in your own region come next. If you can, go with an experienced person. Hikes will make you familiar with places where reptiles and amphibians are found. The best places depend largely on local conditions. Go to ponds and swamps, creeks, ledges, woods and fields. This is the first step in observing or collecting.

**COLLECTING** may seem more important than it is. You can learn much without collecting. Only for the advanced amateur is it necessary to pin down rare species or geographical subspecies for study of body scales, head plates, forms of toes and other details. At that stage systematic collecting is important. If you collect harmless species, turn them loose after you have examined and studied them.

**Hunting Frogs with Headlight**

Snake Collecting Bag

## COLLECTING EQUIPMENT

Snakes and lizards can be carried in muslin bags or pillow cases. When the end is tied, these are safe, and provide enough ventilation. Cans or jars are fine for amphibians. Keep the container half full of moist sphagnum moss for your captive's comfort. A stout net will help you get amphibians, though some collectors prefer to grab by hand. A snake stick will pin down a snake till you can pick it up safely. Some prefer to grab snakes quickly behind the head. Using a stick is safest for a beginner, however. Amateurs should leave poisonous snakes strictly alone. Experience in field trips will help you plan simple but adequate collecting equipment and the proper ways of using such equipment. Remember that a muslin bag can be a death trap for a specimen if left in the sun or in a closed car parked in the open.

Snake Stick and Noose

Terrarium for Frogs

**CAGES AND TANKS** Keep amphibians in aquaria. Some require a rock or float so they can climb out of the water. Others, especially tadpoles, will use any aquaria suitable for fish. Toads will need a moist terrarium; lizards use a cage similar to one for snakes. For snakes and lizards that climb, use a larger cage with a branch set in it. Allow at least a square foot of floor space for a medium-sized snake, more for larger species. Know the habits of the snake. Try, in a simple way, to duplicate the natural habitat. A wooden cage of one-inch boards with a glass front is good; the top should be hinged and used as a door. Three or four one-inch (or larger) holes at the ends and back aid ventilation. These holes should be tightly covered with fine screen. Cover the cage floor with sand or gravel. Add a rock or two and a large enough dish of clean water so that your snake or toad can drink or soak. Be sure that the floor of your cage is always dry. Fasten your water container so a moving snake will not turn it over. Reptiles kept in wet cages often develop skin infections which are difficult to cure. Turn such sick snakes loose.

13

**Amphibian Eggs in Aquarium**

**LIFE HISTORIES** of many amphibians and reptiles are still unknown. Sometimes only the adults have been described, and we know nothing of their eggs or young. Eating habits, wintering habits, and mating habits of many species are still mysteries. A careful, informed amateur may be able to make accurate field observations and records of scientific value. Binoculars are often a help, and a notebook is essential. Field observation may teach you much more than watching animals in a cage. For best results, combine both methods. First study the animals carefully in the field. Then observe them in captivity for further details. The more natural the conditions, the better the observations.

## KEEPING REPTILES AND AMPHIBIANS AS PETS

Collecting reptiles and amphibians to keep as pets is easy. Keeping them alive requires adequate cages, live food, and patience.

**Holding Snake Safely**

Some reptiles and amphibians make good pets, though not intelligent enough to make as good pets as dogs, cats, or even canaries. Some are unusual, most are interesting, but all have their limitations. Turtles are favored. They live long and are easier to feed. Species preferred as pets are noted, but turning these animals loose after you have studied or photographed them is still a good idea. Plan well in advance. Turn your specimens loose or give them to a zoo before you run into difficulties with food or care.

# FIRST AID
# FOR SNAKE BITE

Read this *before* you begin handling snakes.

Snakebites of any kind are rare. They are easily prevented. Wear heavy shoes, boots, or leggings in country where poisonous species are found. Stay on roads, paths, or trails if possible. Step clear of rocks and logs. When climbing rocky ledges, look before you grasp. Finally and most important: no amateur should catch or handle poisonous snakes.

Bites of non-poisonous snakes often leave a U-shaped pattern of tooth marks. Treat them as simple, minor wounds with any good germicide. Bites of poisonous snakes usually show a double puncture caused by the enlarged front fangs. Other teeth marks may be present also. If bitten, try hard to recognize and identify the snake. If the snake is poisonous, complete quiet with prompt first aid, and the use of serum by a doctor, will insure the possibility of complete and rapid recovery.

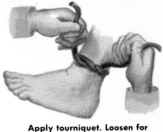

Apply tourniquet. Loosen for 5 min. at 20-min. intervals

Make small incisions.

Suck out poison.

Keep patient quiet, warm, and comfortable.

Phone doctor immediately.

**TURTLES**
(45 U. S. species)

LIZARDS (90 speci..

Scaly Skin

Plated Skin

REPTILES (teeth alike)

**REPTILES**   Though the Age of Reptiles, which flourished for some 120 million years, came to an end about 70 million years ago, many interesting and unusual reptiles are still found today. Some native reptiles occur in every state, though they are more common and more species occur in the warmer parts of this country. Reptiles are classified into four major groups—turtles (45 species), lizards (90 species), snakes (110 species), and alligators and crocodiles (2 species). Reptiles are not always easy to find. Some are small, many are nocturnal, and most are protectively colored.

Reptiles are cold-blooded. A reptile's body temperature is the same as the temperature of its surroundings, except as evaporation lowers it or insolation raises it. Only by behavior is a reptile's temperature controlled. Only on hot sand or rock does a reptile get much warmer than the air. Desert reptiles avoid direct midday sun.

**SNAKES (110 species)**

**CROCODILIANS (2 species)**

**MAMMALS (teeth variable)**

**Hibernation**

Some become dormant (aestivate) in midsummer. In cooler regions reptiles hibernate from late fall to early spring under the soil, rocks, or water. Then they are inactive, sometimes almost lifeless.

All reptiles, even aquatic species, have lungs and breathe air. Their skin is usually covered with scales or plates. Reptilian teeth are commonly uniform in shape and size, lacking the specialization seen in mammals. Most reptiles lay eggs. In a few, the eggs remain inside the mother till ready to hatch. All young are able to care for themselves very soon after birth. Though a few snakes and lizards are poisonous, the great majority of reptiles are harmless. They are often classed as beneficial to man because they feed on rodents and insects. Some reptiles make interesting and unusual pets. All are animals which deserve protection from needless destruction.

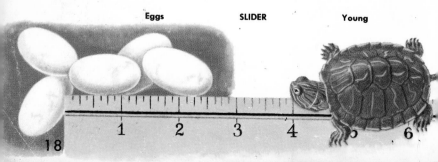

**BOX TURTLE**

**TURTLES** are unusual, ancient reptiles. Their ancestors first appeared some 200 million years ago, long before the dinosaurs. And while those great beasts have long been extinct, turtles with their odd, ungainly form have managed to survive and have remained relatively unchanged for at least 150 million years. Part of the reason for this long survival may be the turtle's unusual skeleton. The top shell or carapace is formed from overgrown, widened ribs. Beneath is the lower shell, or plastron. In the course of their development, turtles have become so modified that their legs are attached within their ribs. This development for protection has made it necessary for turtles to develop longer necks and an unusual way of getting air in and out of their lungs. A turtle's neck forms a tight S-shaped bend, and the curve becomes shallow as the neck extends.

Turtles have no teeth. But their horny bill will tear plant and animal food. Turtles eat insects, worms, grubs, shellfish, fish, and some plants. A few species are

Eggs      SLIDER      Young

largely herbivorous. All turtles lay eggs, usually 6 to 12, and bury them in the ground. Sea Turtles lay many more. Under the heat of the sun these hatch into young which grow to maturity in about 5 to 7 years. Turtles may live longer than any other animals, perhaps up to 150 years. Small species have survived longer than 40 years in captivity.

Male turtles are generally smaller than females; they often have a longer tail, a concave plastron, and long nails on their front feet. In northern sections of the country, turtles hibernate under soil or under mud at the bottom of ponds. Some also become dormant in hot, dry weather. Several kinds are prized as table delicacies. Many make interesting pets that are easy to keep and feed.

Living turtles of North America and adjacent seas fit into seven families. Six are illustrated at the right side of the page by representative species. The seventh family, the land tortoises, is pictured on p. 27. This is the only group correctly called "tortoises."

LEATHERBACK TURTLE

GREEN TURTLE

MUD TURTLE

SNAPPING TURTLE

SOFT-SHELLED TURTLE

FALSE MAP TURTLE

19

**LEATHERBACK TURTLE**

**HAWKSBILL TURTLE**

**SEA TURTLES** are larger than, and different from, pond and land species. The limbs of marine turtles are modified into flippers—streamlined for swimming, clumsy for use on land. As a result, these turtles seldom come ashore, though the female does so to lay her large batch of eggs in late spring. The eggs are buried in the sand just past the high-water mark. Sea Turtles are found in warmer waters of both Atlantic and Pacific, and occasionally off northern shores in summer. Of five kinds, the Leatherback is largest. Specimens

20

**LOGGERHEAD TURTLE**

**GREEN TURTLE**

over 8 ft. long, close to 1,500 lb., have been caught.
The ridged, leathery back makes identification easy.
The Hawksbill, smallest of the Sea Turtles, also is easy
to recognize because of its overlapping scales. This is
the species from which "tortoise shell" comes. The
Green Turtle, most often used for food, has four plates
on each side between the top and the marginal plates.
The Loggerhead Turtle has five plates on each side and
a smaller head than the Green Turtle, with which it may
be confused. It is not as good eating.

**MUSK TURTLES** are aquatic species of ponds, slow streams, and rivers. They often sun themselves in shallow water, but seldom come ashore. The females do so to lay eggs. Note the narrow, high carapace, often covered with algae and water moss. The lower shell  (plastron) is narrow and short, almost like that of Snapping Turtles. The Musk Turtle has a strong odor. Two species occur; the commoner, shown above, has two light stripes on each side of its head.

COMMON MUD TURTLE

YELLOW-NECKED MUD TURTLE

**MUD TURTLES,** five species of them, live about the same as Musk Turtles. They are aquatic, feeding on larvae of water insects and small water animals. Notice that the plastron is much wider in the Mud Turtle and is all scaly. Both ends are hinged, so that the Mud Turtle can pull the plastron in, giving head and limbs more protection. Mud Turtles have a musky odor, too. They are small, rarely over 4 in. long, and are more common in the Southeast.

**COMMON SNAPPER** and its giant relative (see p. 25) are dangerous. Their long necks, powerful jaws, and vicious tempers make them unsafe to handle. Hold them well away from you. Snappers are aquatic, preferring quiet, muddy water. They eat fish and sometimes waterfowl. Notice the sharply toothed rear edge of the rough carapace, which is often coated with green algae. The plastron is small. Adults, 18 in. or more, weigh 20 to 35 lb.

**ALLIGATOR SNAPPER** is the largest fresh-water turtle, reaching a length of 30 in. and a weight of close to 150 lb. Entirely aquatic, it lies on the muddy bottom, its huge mouth agape, wiggling its pink, worm-like tongue to attract an unwary fish. Its powerful jaws can maim a hand or foot. It differs from the Common Snapper in having three high ridges or keels on its back. Specimens are reported to have lived 50 to 60 years and more in zoos.

**SOFT-SHELLED TURTLES** have, in fact, a hard shell, but it is soft-edged and lacks horny scales. These turtles can pull in head and limbs for protection nevertheless. Of two species, one has small bumps or tubercles along the front edge of the carapace; the other does not. Both have long necks, sharp beaks, vicious tempers. Handle them by rear of shell. These turtles grow to a length of about 18 in. and weigh up to 35 lb. They are excellent eating.

26

EASTERN GOPHER TURTLE

**TORTOISES or GOPHER TURTLES** are land turtles with blunt, club-shaped feet very different from the webbed feet of aquatic species. Their diet includes much plant material as well as insects and small animals. Our three species, which differ only in minor ways, are related to the Giant Tortoises of the Galapagos Islands, largest and oldest of land turtles. The relatively high, arched carapace and the habit of digging deep burrows are characteristic.

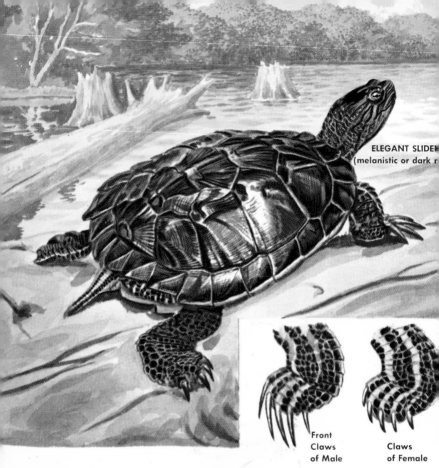

ELEGANT SLIDER
(melanistic or dark r

Front
Claws
of Male

Claws
of Female

**SLIDERS** are a common group of four species. The carapace is usually smooth and fairly flat, the rear edge roughly toothed. The carapace of the Florida and Alabama Sliders arches higher than the carapace of others. The olive-brown shells and skins of Sliders are splotched with red and yellow. The Elegant Slider has a distinctive dash of red behind the eye. The males, much darker than females, were once mistaken for different species. With the extra-long toenails on their front feet they seem to tickle or gently scratch the female's head during courtship. The female later digs

ELEGANT SLIDER

Female and Young

a hole near the shore and deposits about 10 eggs, which she covers with dirt.

All Sliders prefer the quiet waters of rivers and ponds. On warm days they may be found sunning on logs or debris. They are one of the commonest turtles of the Mississippi and its tributaries. Of all young turtles sold in pet shops, Sliders are commonest. They make good pets, live long, and grow to about 1 ft. Painting their shells deforms and may finally kill them.

**SAW-TOOTHED SLIDER** is also called the Hieroglyphic Turtle because the markings on its shell and skin resemble ancient writing. It is a typical Slider with a dark, flattened carapace, 10 to 12 in. long, marked with yellow. The plastron is yellow with dark markings.

Like other Sliders this one feeds on small water animals, insects, and even dead fish; it also eats some water plants. In the various parts of the South, Sliders are prized for their flavor.

**CHICKEN TURTLE** is so called because it is locally eaten despite its size (5 to 8 in.). The brownish carapace has shallow furrows, a smooth rear edge, and thin yellow lines. It is higher and narrower than that of Sliders. The plastron is yellow, as are the undersides of head and limbs, which have thin, dark stripes. Chicken Turtles have very long necks. They prefer ditches and ponds to rivers. More pugnacious than Sliders, they do not make as good pets.

EASTERN PAINTED TURTLE

**PAINTED TURTLES** are perhaps the most common and widespread of turtles. They are found wherever there are ponds, swamps, ditches, or slow streams. These small (5 to 6 in.) turtles spend much of their time in or near water, feeding on water plants, insects, and other small animals. They are also scavengers. In summer, Painted Turtles gather together, and if one approaches quietly, they may be seen sunning on logs, rocks, or even floating water plants. Males are similar

MISSISSIPPI PAINTED TURTLE          WESTERN PAINTED TURTLE

MIDLAND PAINTED TURTLE

to the females but smaller, with the same long nails on their forefeet that Sliders have. Females lay 6 to 12 white eggs in a hole that they have dug laboriously with their hind legs in the soil. The eggs may hatch in two or three months, though some young do not emerge till the following spring. Painted Turtles may be easily identified by their broad, dark, flattened, smooth-edged shells. The margin of the carapace is marked with red; so is the yellow-streaked skin, especially on head and limbs. The plastron is yellow, sometimes being tinted with red. In all four subspecies of Painted Turtles the upper jaw is notched in front. The notch has a small projection on each side. Markings and details of carapace and plastron differ from subspecies to subspecies. Painted Turtles are shy and are not easily captured. They make good pets but must be fed in water. Young Painted Turtles will attack fish if they are put in an aquarium with them.

FALSE MAP TURTLE

**MAP TURTLES** are aquatic turtles often found in large numbers in ponds, swamps, and quiet streams. They are even more timid than Painted Turtles. Dozens may be sunning on a log, but at the least disturbing noise they instantly drop back into the water. Like Sliders, these turtles are captured and sold for food. Of the five species, the False Map Turtle is reported better eating. The young of both make fair pets, feeding on chopped meat and earthworms. At full growth they are 9 to 12 in. long. Adults, having strong jaws, feed on

snails, clams, insects, and other water animals. The female, coming ashore briefly in early summer to lay 10 to 16 white eggs, returns to the water as soon as the eggs are buried. Map turtles are named for the faint, yellow pattern on the carapace. The lines are brighter on the head and limbs. The keeled carapace and its roughly toothed rear edge are identification marks. Males, smaller than females, may be weaker, more timid.

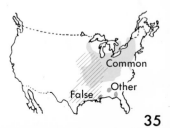

35

**BLANDING TURTLE** with its hinged plastron somewhat resembles the Box Turtle, but cannot close its shell tightly. It has webbed feet and lacks the hooked bill of the Box Turtle. The plastron is notched at the back. Blanding Turtle, 7 to 8 in. long, prefers water,

but it also lives in marshes, where it feeds on insects, worms, and various plants. This shy turtle tames easily and will make a good pet if kept in a large, shallow pan of water.

**TERRAPIN,** often called Diamondback because of the angular rings on the carapace plate, is the best-known eating turtle. It is raised on turtle farms, and 8-in. specimens sell for as high as $10. Young are protected by law in Maryland and North Carolina. These turtles of brackish water and tide-water streams have webbed feet. The carapace is dull olive, the plastron yellow. Markings vary. Females are larger. Food: small shellfish, crabs, worms, plants.

37

**EASTERN BOX TURTLE**

**BOX TURTLES** are land species, occasionally found in or near water, though they are well adapted for life on land. They prefer moist, open woods or swamps and feed on insects, earthworms, snails, fruits, and berries. Box Turtles have a hinged plastron which they pull tight against the carapace for complete protection when they are frightened. The carapace, 4 to 5 in. long, is highly arched. Of the two species of Box Turtles, Eastern and Western, the former is divided into several subspecies, distinguished by the shape and markings on the shells and by the number of toes

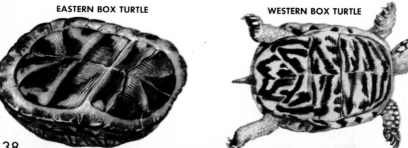

**EASTERN BOX TURTLE**       **WESTERN BOX TURTLE**

38

WESTERN BOX TURTLE

(three or four) on the hind feet. The plastron of the female is usually flat; that of the male, curved inward. Males have longer tails, and the eye of the male is usually bright red. The female has dark reddish or brown eyes. In early summer the female buries four or five round, white eggs in a sunny spot. These hatch in about three months. The young may hibernate soon after, without feeding. Young Box Turtles grow ½ to ¾ in. yearly for five or six years; then they grow slower—about ¼ in. a year. At 5 years they mate and lay eggs; at 20 they are full-grown, and they may live to be as old as 80. Box Turtles have been reported living 25 years and more in captivity. They make fine pets and may be kept in a fenced outdoor pen or allowed to roam around the house. In captivity, they eat meat and a variety of fruits and greens.

Western

Eastern

39

**SPOTTED TURTLE** is a small (3 to 5 in.) common turtle with round orange or yellow spots on its smooth, black carapace. The head is colored similarly. Living in quiet fresh water, this turtle feeds on aquatic insects, tadpoles, and dead fish, but eats only when in water. It

makes an excellent, long-lived pet. Feed it meat, fish, and bits of lettuce. The tail of the male is about twice as long as that of the female.

**PACIFIC TURTLE** is related and similar to the Eastern Spotted Turtle, but is larger—6 to 7 in. The yellow dots and streaks on the carapace are faint. The plastron, concave on the male, is yellow with dark patches at the edges. This is the only fresh-water turtle of the far West. Living in mountain lakes and in slow stretches of streams, Pacific Turtles feed on small water life, including some plants. They make good pets.

41

**MUHLENBERG TURTLE** is quickly identified by the large orange spot on each side of the head. The dark carapace is short (3 to 4 in.) and narrow, marked with concentric rings. This turtle is semi-aquatic, living in swamps but returning to water when in danger and

sometimes to feed. The male has a longer tail. Muhlenberg Turtle makes an excellent pet, eating chopped meat, earthworms, fruits, and greens. It does not have to be fed in water, as do Spotted Turtles.

**WOOD TURTLE** is recognized easily by its bright, orange-red skin and its heavy, keeled carapace with deep concentric grooves. Adults are 7 to 9 in. long. They prefer moist woods, though they move into open land to feed and, when it is dry, to swamps and into ponds and slow streams. They make fine pets and will take fruit, berries and bits of meat from your hand. The male has heavier, longer claws, and larger plates on its fore-limbs.

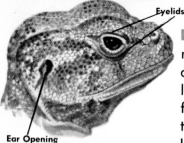

Eyelids

Ear Opening

**LIZARDS** are more like ancient reptiles than either snakes or alligators are. Bones of fossil lizards have been found in rocks formed during the period when the dinosaurs were common. Lizards are found mainly in the warmer parts of the world, though a few species live as far north as Canada and Finland. Over 2,500 species are known. These have been grouped into about 20 families, 9 of which occur in the United States. About 350 species are found in North America; 90 of these occur within the boundaries of the United States.

A few species of lizards (pp. 67-68) are snake-like in appearance; they have long bodies and have lost all traces of legs. In all other characteristics, however, they resemble other normal lizards, and close observation easily distinguishes them from snakes. Lizards are typically four-legged, with five toes on each foot. They have scaly skins. On the underside the scales form several or many rows, in contrast to snakes, which have only a single row of scales.

Salamanders (pp. 137-153) are sometimes mistaken for lizards. Salamanders have smooth skins, live in moist places, have less than five toes on the front feet.

Lizards usually have movable eyelids (snakes have not) and an ear opening on the side of the head. Most

**Belly Scales—LIZARDS**

**Belly Scales—SNAKES**

lay eggs, though in a few cases the eggs develop inside the mother's body and the young are born alive. The males and females are alike in many species; in other species they are different in size and color. Many lizards feed on insects and other small animals, such as those illustrated on this page, but a few species feed on plant material. They recognize their prey by its movement and grasp it with lightning-like speed. Lizards can run rapidly—the fastest has been clocked at about 15 miles per hour. Most can swim. Some desert species move through the sand just below the surface with a swimming movement.

Lizards are not easily caught, but those that are make reasonably good pets. They can be kept in terraria or wire cages. Cover the bottom of the cage with a heavy layer of sand; set a dish of water and a few rocks in it. Feed lizards mealworms, flies, small earthworms, or other live food. Anoles and Horned Lizards are common pets; others may eat better, however. Leave the venomous Gila-monster (p. 69) alone, even though it may not be so dangerous as poisonous snakes.

CENTIPEDE

FLY

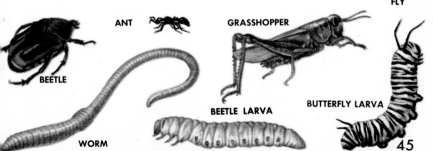

ANT

GRASSHOPPER

BEETLE

BEETLE LARVA

BUTTERFLY LARVA

WORM

45

TUBERCULAR GECKO

**GECKOS** are unusually attractive lizards, recognized by their large, often lidless eyes with vertical pupils. The skin, usually covered with fine, beaded scales, is almost transparent. Most have enlarged, padded toes. Geckos live around houses or on trees, feeding on small insects. They are nocturnal. Geckos lay two to three or more small white eggs with brittle shells during summer. Some tropical species have become naturalized in Florida. Geckos are docile and rarely bite. Their tails break off easily. Tubercular and Ground Geckos are our only native species. The Least Gecko probably came to Florida from the West Indies, while the Turkish Gecko originally came from North Africa.

LEAST GECKO

TURKISH GECKO

WESTERN GROUND GECKO

**GROUND GECKOS** (2 similar species) are western lizards (4 to 5 in. long). Tails are about half the body length but have usually broken and regrown shorter. Ground Geckos live in rocky or sandy deserts and lower mountain slopes. They come out at night to feed on small insects and, in turn, are eaten by snakes and larger lizards. They hibernate from Oct. to May but are common other months. They never bite, tame quickly and do well in captivity.

Other Geckos

Ground

Tuber-cular

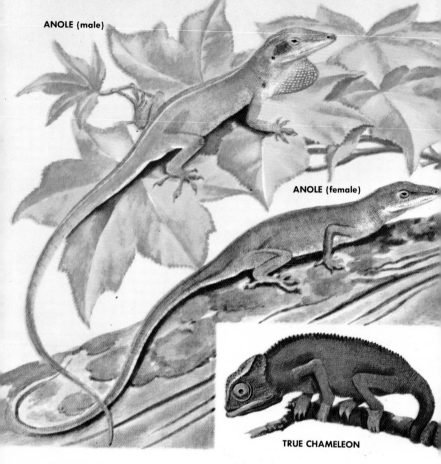

ANOLE (male)

ANOLE (female)

TRUE CHAMELEON

**ANOLE or AMERICAN CHAMELEON,** common and attractive, can change color, often matching its background of leaves or branches, where it feasts on insects. This is the "chameleon" sold at fairs and circuses. Kept as a pet, it needs live food. Anoles will lap up water sprinkled on plants. Males have a flap of skin on their throat. Eggs (two or three), laid in summer under moist debris, hatch in about six weeks. True chameleons are Old World lizards.

**CHUCKWALLA** (16 in. long) is, next to the Gila-monster (p. 69), our largest lizard. It feeds on flowers and fruit of cactus and tender parts of desert plants, and usually eats well in captivity. Chuckwallas sun themselves on rocks but, when disturbed, dart into crevices, where they inflate their bodies and are difficult to remove. Indians used to eat them. The young have bands across body and tail; the adults have tail bands only.

49

**DESERT IGUANA or CRESTED LIZARD,** a handsome spotted species of open deserts, lives in burrows under sparse shrubs. Entirely vegetarian, it feeds on tender desert plants. Desert Iguana is fairly large (12 to 15 in.), but its tail is almost twice its body length. It runs rapidly, is wary and hard to catch. Each has its own territory for feeding; here the female lays her eggs. Males have a reddish patch on each side of the tail.

50

TRUE IGUANA

SPINY IGUANA

**SPINY and TRUE IGUANA,** representing two groups of large American lizards, are not found in the United States, but come to within 100 miles of our border. They are often seen in zoos. About 10 or 11 species of Spiny or False Iguana (1 to 4 ft. long) live on the ground in lower California, Mexico, and farther south into Central America. The True Iguana (4 to 6 ft. long) lives in tropical trees. Both are favorite foods of the Indians. Both Spiny and True Iguanas are herbivorous. Other Iguanas live in the Galapagos Islands and West Indies.

51

COLLARED LIZARD

## COLLARED and LEOPARD LIZARD
The black collar marks the Collared Lizard; so does its long tail, plump body, thin neck, and relatively large head. Males are more brightly colored, with a tinge of orange and yellow. The body is 4 to 5 in. long; the tail twice that. Collared Lizards, fairly common in rocky areas, feed on insects and small lizards. Wary, they can run swiftly on their hind legs. Collared Lizards bite when captured and do not live well when caged. A species of the lower Rio Grande valley, not well known, lacks the black collar. The Leopard Lizard,

**LEOPARD LIZARD**

somewhat like the Collared Lizard in form and size, is more spotted and has a narrower head and body. It prefers flat, sandy areas with some vegetation. As food it takes insects and lizards, and often eats its own kind. Oddly, females develop a deep salmon color on their undersides at the close of the breeding season. They lay 2 to 4 eggs, which hatch in a month or so. Because Leopard Lizards are vicious, they do not make satisfactory pets.

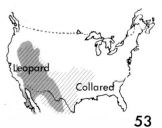

Leopard

Collared

53

CLIMBING UTA

**CLIMBING and GROUND UTAS** are related groups. The former prefer trees and rocks, where their dull color gives protection. Their irregular-sized scales are a field characteristic. Males are pale blue on the underside near the back legs; females lack this color. The adults are small (5 to 6 in.). Ground Utas are small striped or speckled lizards living in rocky places and feeding on small insects. These very common lizards vary somewhat with their surroundings. Both Climbing and Ground Utas are relatively easy to catch at night, when they are less active than in the daytime.

Ground

Climbing

Collared (red)

GROUND UTA

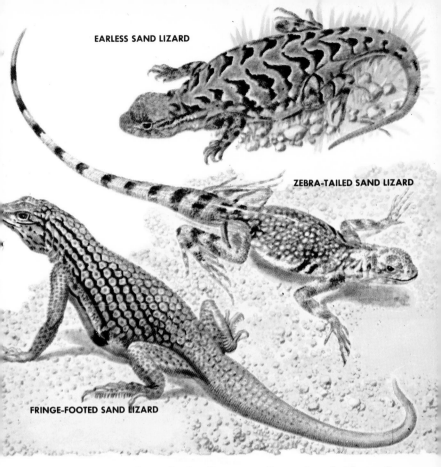

**EARLESS SAND LIZARD**

**ZEBRA-TAILED SAND LIZARD**

**FRINGE-FOOTED SAND LIZARD**

**SAND LIZARDS** include five medium-sized (6 to 8 in.) lizards all preferring sandy terrain. Two of the species illustrated are at their best in the sand dunes of the California and Arizona deserts. All have a skin fold across the underside, in front of the forelegs. Legs and toes are long. Tails are about body length and are often marked with black bars underneath. Sand Lizards are active and not easily caught. They all feed on small insects.

Zebra-tailed

Earless

Fringe-footed

55

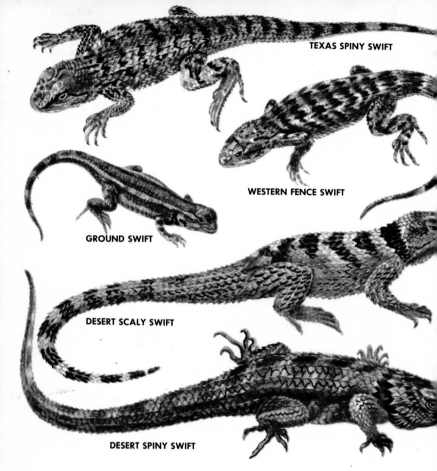

**TEXAS SPINY SWIFT**

**WESTERN FENCE SWIFT**

**GROUND SWIFT**

**DESERT SCALY SWIFT**

**DESERT SPINY SWIFT**

**SWIFTS** form a large group of common lizards, including Fence, Spiny, and Scaly Lizards. Some 30 forms (species and subspecies) live in the United States, almost three times as many farther south. The largest have bodies about 5 in. long, tails slightly longer. All are active in daylight, spending the night in cracks, crevices, or on branches. Some species lay eggs; others bear 6 to 12 young alive. Head, body, and limb forms are guides to the entire Swift group, once you learn them. These lizards lack the skin fold across

Underview

ch of Eggs

EASTERN FENCE SWIFT

the throat that Sand Lizards (p. 55) and similar species have. Some Swifts are blue or blue-patched on the undersides; this is more pronounced in males. Detailed identification may be difficult. Swifts, good climbers, are often found in trees, on boulders, among rocks. True to their name, they are hard to catch. Their food is mainly small insects. They do well in captivity if given live food but are not especially good pets.

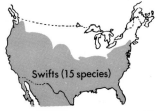

Swifts (15 species)

SHORT-HORNED LIZARD

**HORNED LIZARDS** are unique. These odd, flattened creatures are found only in the West and in Mexico. The only other lizard like them is one in Australia. Most have various-sized spines on the head which give the group its name. Eight species are found in dry, sandy areas, where they lie on rocks or half buried in the sand. When an insect appears, a quick snap of the lizard's tongue takes care of it. Some species lay 20 to 30 eggs; in others up to a dozen young are born alive. In one species eggs hatch in only a few hours; others take several weeks. These unusual liz-

58

TEXAS HORNED LIZARD

Underground Clutch of Eggs

ards may squirt a thin stream of blood from the corners of their eyes when frightened. Some puff up when angered; others flatten themselves out even more. They are easily captured, can be safely handled, and become tame. In captivity they will do well if given live insects and moist leaves from which they can lap up the water they need. Ants are among their favorite foods. These lizards must be kept warm (at least 70 degrees) or they will not eat.

59

GRANITE NIGHT LIZARD

ARIZONA NIGHT LIZARD

**NIGHT LIZARDS** are mottled, medium-sized lizards. Both body and tail are about 3 in. long. They live in areas of granite, behind the loose-scaled flakes of rock or under fallen stalks of yucca. Note the vertical pupil in the eye and lack of eye-lids. Horizontal rows of

plates cross the belly. The four kinds are nocturnal, spending the day in sheltered cracks. Young (two or three at a time) are born alive. The food is beetles and other small insects.

**SKINKS** Some 20 species of Skinks are found in the United States; no other lizards have so wide a range. They are the only lizards that many people in the North have ever seen. All are small to moderate in size. The body length is not usually more than 5 in., the tail not much over 6 in. Most Skinks are smaller. Skinks can be recognized by their smooth, flat scales, which produce a glossy, silky appearance. Most have short legs, and in one (p. 64) the legs are degenerate, but most are swift runners. All burrow occasionally, for Skinks, in general, are ground lizards. Active during warm days, Skinks feed mainly on insects, spiders, worms, and perhaps small vertebrates. They hibernate all winter in the ground or under logs. The most common Skink mates during May. Eggs, 6 to 18, are laid about six weeks later. The mother spends the next six or seven weeks brooding her eggs till they hatch, something unusual for lizards. The young are only about an inch long.

Skinks can be roughly identified by the markings on their backs. Most common in the East are the five-lined Skinks, which have five light lines from head to tail. Lines are clearer in younger animals. In the West, four-lined Skinks are common. Other Skinks have eight lines, two lines, or no lines at all. They are not easily caught but will do well in captivity if live food—mealworms, ant larvae, or beetle grubs—are available. Keep in a terrarium with rocks under which they can hide.

Skinks
(20 species)

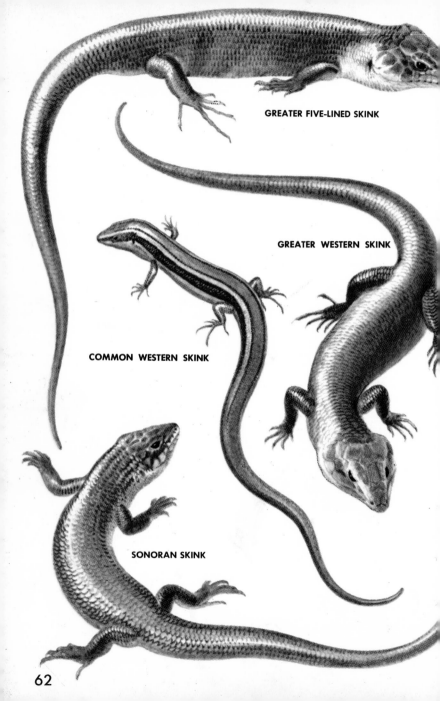

GREATER FIVE-LINED SKINK

GREATER WESTERN SKINK

COMMON WESTERN SKINK

SONORAN SKINK

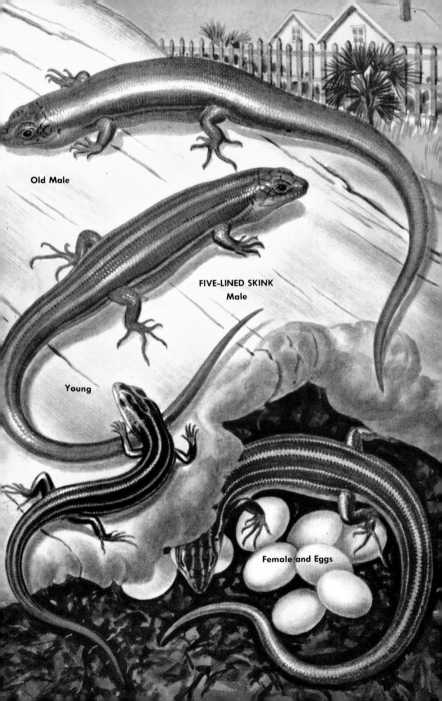

**Old Male**

**FIVE-LINED SKINK**
**Male**

**Young**

**Female and Eggs**

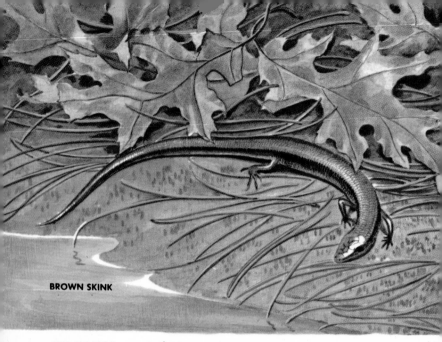

**BROWN SKINK**

**BROWN and SAND SKINKS** are similar to the other skinks just noted. The Brown Skink (2 in. long, with longer tail) has a transparent disk in the eyelid. Notable also are the smooth, flat scales and the broad, brown bands down the sides. This skink prefers wooded moist places; it lays its eggs in humus or rotted wood. It is an active lizard, most commonly found on the ground, often hiding under leaves. The Sand Skink is a burrowing lizard about 2 in. long, with legs small and degenerate, especially the forelegs. No other lizard has legs quite like it. It is found in pine woods, in dry or sandy soils.

**SAND SKINK**

Brown

Sand

SIX-LINED WHIPTAIL LIZARD

TIGER WHIPTAIL LIZARD

**WHIPTAIL LIZARDS** or Racerunners, a very diverse group, give the experts trouble. One of the most common and widespread is the 6-lined species, somewhat skink-like in appearance. Its body length is about 3 in.; tail at least twice as long. These lizards are found in many dry localities, feeding during the day on insects, worms, and snails. Other Whiptails are checkered or spotted. They are more common in the West.

65

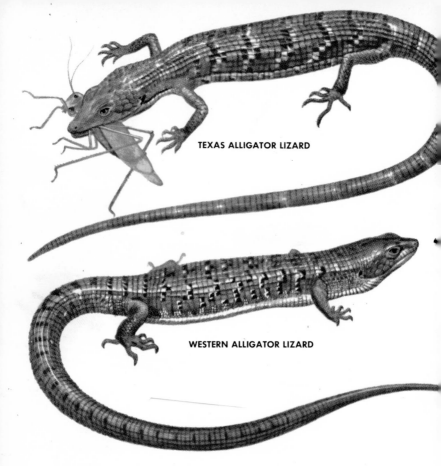

TEXAS ALLIGATOR LIZARD

WESTERN ALLIGATOR LIZARD

**ALLIGATOR LIZARDS,** named for their shape and heavy scales, are slow, dull-colored, solitary, with a banded or speckled back. They are fairly large (10 in.). Some species lay eggs; in others the 2 to 15 young are born alive. They feed on insects and spiders and,  in turn, are the food of larger reptiles, mammals, and birds. Alligator Lizards do well in captivity, but they fight when several are in a cage together. Males may bite painfully.

**GLASS-SNAKE LIZARDS** are of three closely similar species—limbless, somewhat snakelike, 2 to 3 ft. long. Ear openings, eyelids, and many rows of belly scales proclaim them to be true lizards. The very long tail breaks off more easily than that of other lizards. It may break off when the animal is cap-tured or roughly handled. The tail, of course, cannot rejoin the body, but a new, shorter tail grows in its place. These lizards feed on insects. They may bite when handled.

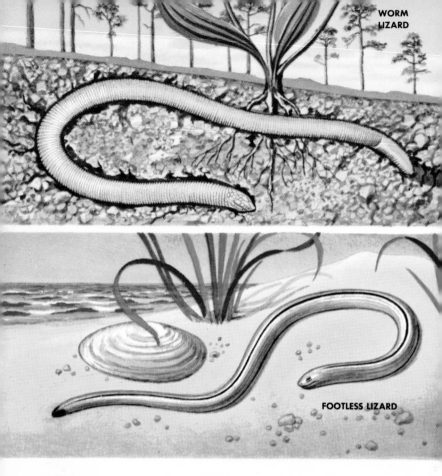

WORM
LIZARD

FOOTLESS LIZARD

**WORM and FOOTLESS LIZARDS** are two small burrowing species. The former (up to 10 in. long, only ¼ in.
thick), found in sandy soil of pine woods, has distinct
rings which make it look much like a large earthworm.
It is limbless, earless, and blind. The Footless Lizard of
California, which is even smaller
(6 in.), has small eyes but is earless and limbless. Two forms occur,
one of which is silvery, the other
black. These lizards depend on
small insects for their food.

Footless

Worm

**GILA-MONSTER,** our only poisonous lizard, grows up to 2 ft. long. The poison, from modified salivary glands in the lower jaw, is not injected and may not enter the wound when the lizard bites. Usually slow and clumsy, Gila-monsters can twist their heads, bite swiftly, and hang on strongly. Leave them to the experts. Gila-monsters live under rocks and in burrows by day. They feed on eggs, mice, and other lizards. The 6 to 12 eggs hatch in about a month.

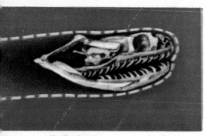

Skull of Non-poisonous Snake—
Eastern Racer

Skull of Poisonous Snake—
Cottonmouth

**SNAKES** are the best-known reptiles. Of some 250 species and subspecies found in the U.S., 36 produce poison which can harm man. In few places are poisonous snakes common, and death from snake bite is a rarity. All snakes except Blind Snakes have large scales across the belly. Besides lacking limbs, they also lack ear openings and eyelids that move. Each side of the snake's lower jaw moves separately, enabling it to swallow prey larger than its normal mouth size. Teeth are small and hooked. The larger fangs of poisonous species are grooved or hollow.

The snake's long, forked tongue is harmless. It serves as a simple kind of feeler and "smeller." The tongue cannot smell but does bring odorous particles into the mouth and into contact with smell-sensitive organs there. These supplement the sensations the snake receives

Copperhead Shedding

Head of Scarlet King
Snake (showing tongue
attachment and teeth)

Eggs of Red King Snake

Copperhead at Birth

through its nostrils. Snakes do not hear as we do; their entire body picks up vibrations through the ground. The eyesight of snakes is fairly good, though their eyes are not as well adjusted for distance as ours. Some can see very well at night.

Snakes feed on live animals: insects, worms, frogs, mice, rats, and rabbits — mostly animals harmful to man. Some snakes lay eggs; the young of others are born alive. Snakes may have about a dozen young at a time and occasionally as many as 99. The mother gives them no care after birth; the young fend for themselves and grow rapidly. Most of them double their size in one year and are full grown in two or three years. In growing, snakes shed their skins at least once and often several times a year.

Although snakes are kept as pets by some people, they are not very intelligent. They are unusual, attractive—even beautiful. Some species are easy to tame and never attempt to bite. Only a few will eat well in captivity. Live food is usually needed.

Shed Skin

71

**BLIND SNAKES,** sometimes called Worm Snakes because of their color and size (8 to 12 in.), are truly blind. They may come to the surface at night. Most are found under stones or in digging. They eat worms and insect larvae. Captive specimens never bite. They bur-

row rapidly when sand or soil is put in the cage. The three similar species are the only American snakes without large belly scales. Blind Snakes lay eggs. They are relatives of the Boas.

RUBBER BOA

ROSY BOA

**BOAS** are not all large tropical snakes. Two species live north of Mexico. The Rosy or California Boa, an attractive, docile, small-scaled constrictor, makes a fine pet. It lives in dry, rocky foothills, feeding mainly on rodents. The grayish Rubber Boa, also heavy-bodied, has a short, blunt tail which it displays like a head while its real head is protected by the coils of its body. It grows up to 2 ft. long; the Rosy Boa is larger (3 ft.). Both bear live young.

Rubber

Rosy

**RAINBOW SNAKE** is a handsome species. Stripes vary from orange to red. The underside is red with a double row of black spots. This snake of swampy regions often burrows and is not commonly seen. It is smaller (40 in.) than the closely related Mud Snake  (p. 75) and like it has a sharp "spine" at the end of its tail. Little is known of its life history and feeding habits. The female lays 20 or more eggs, which hatch in about 60 days.

**MUD SNAKES** (two similar forms) are the subject of many superstitions. The spike or stinger on the tail is said to be poisonous. This snake, also called Hoop Snake, is supposed to grasp its tail in its mouth and roll down the road. Such tales about the harmless, attractive, small-headed Mud Snakes are untrue. These burrowing swamp snakes feed on fish and frogs, especially on Sirens and Congo-eels (pp. 139-140). Length, 4 to 6 ft.; lays 20 to 80 or more eggs.

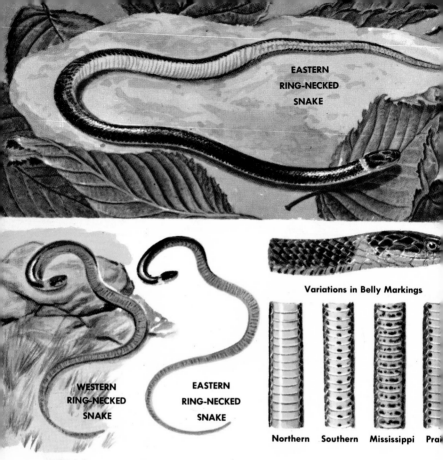

EASTERN
RING-NECKED
SNAKE

WESTERN
RING-NECKED
SNAKE

EASTERN
RING-NECKED
SNAKE

Variations in Belly Markings

Northern  Southern  Mississippi  Prai

**RING-NECKED SNAKES** (three species) are small (12 to 18 in.), common, attractive snakes living in moist woods under rocks or fallen logs, where they feed on small insects and worms. They lay eggs which hatch in about two months. Recognize these snakes by their slate-gray color and the yellow-to-orange ring behind the head. The underside is yellow, orange, or red, sometimes spotted. They may secrete a smelly fluid when captured, but soon tame. Captives eat poorly.

KEELED GREEN SNAKE

eled Scale

SMOOTH-SCALED GREEN SNAKE

**GREEN SNAKES,** slender and harmless, live in greenery where they are hard to see. The smaller species (15 to 18 in.) with smooth scales prefers open grassy places. The other, which grows twice as long, has a rough appearance due to a ridge or keel on each scale. Often found in bushes and vines, this one feeds on insects. Eggs of both species hatch into dark young which gradually turn green. Green Snakes are docile, but as neither eats well, they languish in captivity.

Smooth

Rough

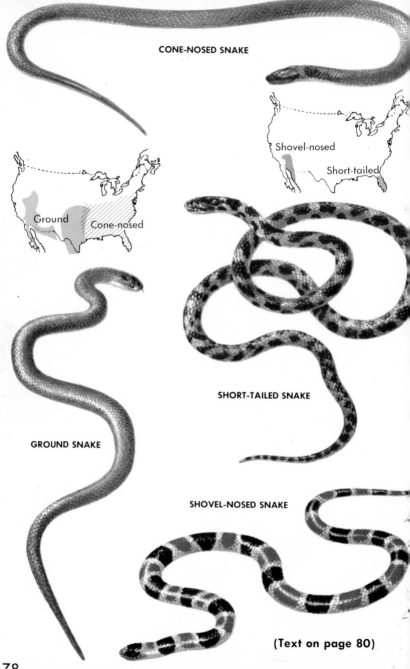

CONE-NOSED SNAKE

Shovel-nosed

Short-tailed

Ground

Cone-nosed

SHORT-TAILED SNAKE

GROUND SNAKE

SHOVEL-NOSED SNAKE

(Text on page 80)

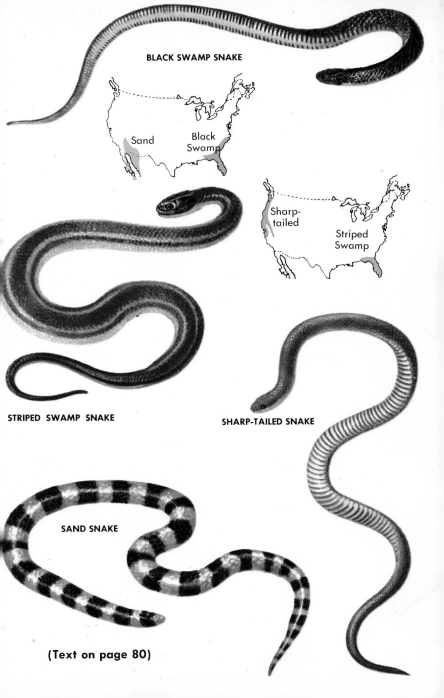

BLACK SWAMP SNAKE

Sand · Black Swamp

Sharp-tailed · Striped Swamp

STRIPED SWAMP SNAKE

SHARP-TAILED SNAKE

SAND SNAKE

(Text on page 80)

## SMALLER, LESS COMMON, HARMLESS SNAKES
**( Illustrations on Pages 78 and 79)**

**CONE-NOSED SNAKES** (10 to 12 in.) are two wood-land species also called Ground Snakes. Brownish or gray above; some with small black dots. Food: small insects and worms. Young are born alive.

**SHORT-TAILED SNAKE** (18 to 24 in.) is like a small Red King Snake. An aggressive, burrowing, upland snake, it kills small prey, often other snakes, by constriction. Tail is very short.

**GROUND SNAKES** (10 to 15 in.) are two small banded species of variable color and pattern, similar but not related to Sharp-tailed. Food: insects, spiders, etc.

**SHOVEL-NOSED SNAKE** (12 to 16 in.) is a ground snake (two species) slightly larger than Ground Snakes and related to them. Snout projecting but flattened. A yellowish, egg-laying sand burrower.

**BLACK SWAMP SNAKE** (12 to 16 in.) is thick-bodied, red-bellied, swamp-loving. Black bar on each belly scale. Young born alive. Food: probably fish, frogs.

**STRIPED SWAMP SNAKE** (18 to 24 in.) is aquatic, living in holes and tunnels along ditches and in swamps. Food: mainly crayfish and frogs. Young are born alive.

**SHARP-TAILED SNAKE** (12 to 16 in.) is somewhat stout. Little is known of its habits. Note the light yellow stripe on sides, black bands on yellow belly scales.

**SAND SNAKE** (10 to 14 in.) is a burrower in desert sands. Crawls just below the surface, aided by a broad, heavy snout. Yellow to red, with dark bands almost encircling body. Scales small and shiny. Life history largely unknown. Said to eat ant larvae.

WESTERN HOG-NOSED SNAKE

COMMON HOG-NOSED SNAKE

**HOG-NOSED SNAKE** is unique and amusing. When molested, it hisses, spreads, and strikes, as though to appear dangerous, but it never bites. If threats fail, it rolls over and plays dead. Because of its ferocious puffing, this harmless snake is sometimes called Puff Adder. The hard, turned-up nose helps in burrowing after toads, which are the preferred food of these snakes, often making up their entire diet. The Hog-nosed Snake lays about two dozen eggs in summer. They are gentle snakes and do well in captivity, if toads are available as food. Three similar species, all heavily built. Common Hog-nosed Snake, 2 to 3 ft. long, is the largest.

VINE SNAKE

WESTERN HOOK-NOSED SNAKE

WESTERN HOOK-NOSED SNAKE

FANGED NIGHT SNAKE

Western
Hook-nosed

Fanged
Night

Vine

Black-striped

(Text on Page 84)

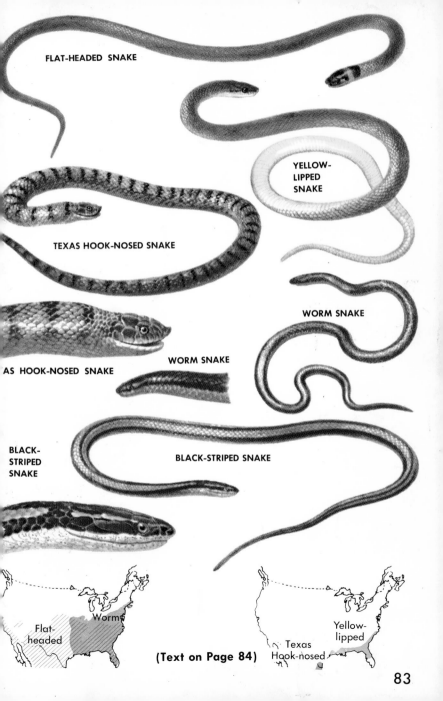

FLAT-HEADED SNAKE

YELLOW-LIPPED SNAKE

TEXAS HOOK-NOSED SNAKE

WORM SNAKE

AS HOOK-NOSED SNAKE

WORM SNAKE

BLACK-STRIPED SNAKE

BLACK-STRIPED SNAKE

Flat-headed

Worm

Yellow-lipped

Texas Hook-nosed

(Text on Page 84)

83

**(Illustrations on Pages 82–83)**

**VINE SNAKE*** (to 4 ft. or more) is a bush-dweller of semi-arid regions, very slender. Longer, narrower head than other American snakes. Reddish-brown; white line down belly. Food: lizards.

**WESTERN HOOK-NOSED SNAKE** is a blotched, egg-laying burrower resembling a miniature Hog-nosed Snake (10 to 12 in.) but is not kin.

**FANGED NIGHT SNAKE*** (to 30 in.), wide-headed, slender, is an egg-layer. It feeds on both invertebrates and small vertebrates. Often found in trees and bushes.

**FLAT-HEADED SNAKES*** (12 to 14 in.) are a large group of secretive or burrowing, egg-laying species. All but one have a black head cap.

**YELLOW-LIPPED SNAKE** (12 to 16 in.) has a yellow upper lip. Back reddish-brown, belly yellow. An egg-layer of swamps, found under logs and debris. Food: frogs, toads, insects.

**TEXAS HOOK-NOSED SNAKE** (10 to 12 in.), related to the Western, is sub-tropical, with a larger shovel-snout than the Western but with similar habits. Ashy gray with gray and black cross bands.

**WORM SNAKE** (10 to 13 in.), widely occurring, is a burrower, rarely seen. Shiny, smooth scales. An egg-layer; feeds on earthworms. Found in woods.

**BLACK-STRIPED SNAKE*** (16 to 20 in.) is a night snake. Feeds on frogs, toads, lizards. An egg-layer and ground-dweller. Rare; more common in tropical America.

* Species with weak venom and small, fixed, grooved fangs in rear of upper jaw.

**WESTERN RACER**

**EASTERN RACER**

**RACERS** are aggressive and graceful. Eastern forms, averaging 4 ft., are smooth, blue-black, with white chin and throat. Western form, smaller, is greenish or yellowish brown, belly and chin lighter. Both are very active, at home in bushes and trees. Food: small mammals, birds, insects, frogs, lizards, other snakes. Tropic Racer, speckled, occurs only in southern tip of Texas.

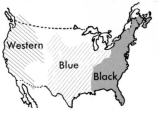

**YOUNG RACER**

**COACHWHIP and WHIPSNAKES** are closely related to the Racers, but thinner and longer. Those illustrated represent two groups—one typical of the East, one of the West. The former are a variable brown (some are red or pinkish), darker at the head, becoming lighter toward the tail. Coachwhip is the largest of the group; some over 7 ft. long have been reported. Western species are usually 4 to 5 ft. long. These are typically striped with yellow on the sides against a dark back; the belly is usually lighter. Several of these are desert forms, but all are active during the day.

WHIPSNAKE

All are alert and fast. They feed on mice, lizards, and small snakes, moving rapidly over sand or through brush after their prey. They do not kill by constriction, as some people believe. Too swift to be caught easily, when they are caught these snakes will strike and will thrash their thin, long tails rapidly. They never tame enough to make good pets. Eight to 12 eggs are laid in early summer, each about 1 by 1½ in. Four species of these snakes live in this country.

Whipsnakes

Coachwhip Snake

**PATCH-NOSED SNAKES,** relatives (three species) of Racers (p. 85), are as fast and active. On the move day or night, they like any terrain. The blunt shield over the nose plus the yellow and brown stripes down the snake's back give positive identification. Adults are about 3 ft. long. Lizards and other small desert life are eaten. Females lay eggs. The nose may help in burrowing in sand. Rear teeth are enlarged but venom seems absent.

**LEAF-NOSED SNAKES,** small relatives of the Patch-noses, have an even more exaggerated nosepiece. Once considered very rare, they are fairly common in the deserts at night. The two species are marked by dark blotches. Both are moderately stout, 12 to 15 in. long. They are pugnacious, coiling and striking when caught, but are harmless. They are egg-layers, and are reported to feed on desert lizards or lizard eggs.

**GRAY RAT SNAKE**

**RAT SNAKES** include five large species, common and widely distributed in the East and Middle West. The colors differ from species to species, making identification easier. All are fast, active snakes. When caught they may bite freely and excrete a foul-smelling fluid from glands at the base of the tail. They tend to tame down in captivity and make fair pets. All rat snakes are constrictors. Members of this group have been known by diverse common names which are often misleading. Names used here are truer to the snakes. The Black Rat Snake, also known as the Pilot Black

**YELLOW RAT SNAKE**

BLACK RAT SNAKE (adult)

Snake, may be mistaken for the Black Racer (p. 85). The Black Rat Snake has some scales tipped with white —remains of a pattern of blotches seen more clearly in the young of all members of this group. The scales are slightly keeled; those of the Black Racer are not. The Gray Rat Snake, a more southern form, has blotches of gray or brown against a lighter background. The Yellow Rat Snake (Striped Chicken Snake) averages 4 to 5 ft. long and may sometimes reach 7 ft. It is dull or olive yellow with four black lines down its back. Often found around barns and stables, it is looking for rats more often than for fowl.

BLACK RAT SNAKE (young)

Other Rat Snakes

Common Rat Snake

**CORN and FOX SNAKES** are more colorful members of the rat snake group. Corn Snake (often found in corn fields) is better known as Red Rat Snake because of the reddish-brown or crimson blotches against the lighter background. A very similar western form lacks the red color. Red Rat Snake does not grow as large as Yellow Rat Snake but it exhibits (as do the others) a pattern of hissing and vibrating its sharp tail when cornered or molested. The Fox Snake has the same build as the other rat snakes but is somewhat heavier. It av-

**FOX SNAKE**

erages 3 to 4 ft. long, with brownish blotches against a straw-yellow base color. Found in woods and open country, it is less of a climber than other rat snakes. All rat snakes lay eggs, often in rotted logs or stumps. The young, blotched in color, may differ much from adults. Red Rat Snake and Fox Snake are reported to tame better, to feed better in captivity, and to make better pets than other members of the group.

Fox Snake

Corn Snakes and kin

93

**INDIGO SNAKES** 8 ft. long have been reported. Thus they are among the largest North American snakes. Related South American forms are even larger. This heavy, handsome, shiny, midnight-blue, fast racer feeds on small mammals and other snakes. It is often

found in burrows of gophers or rabbits. The Indigo Snake tames easily in captivity, and does well if it can be made to eat. This is the harmless snake that "snake charmers" at the circus often handle.

**GLOSSY or FADED SNAKE** is related and somewhat similar to the Bull Snakes (p. 96). It has smooth scales, while Bull Snakes are keeled. These smooth, shiny scales are responsible for the Glossy Snake's common name. Blotched, spotted, and gray-brown, these snakes are slender, with narrow heads. They are constrictors, feeding on lizards, rodents, and other small animals. They lay eggs and are nocturnal. Adults average 30 to 36 in. long.

**PINE SNAKE**

**Pine Snake Eggs**

**BULL SNAKES** are found from coast to coast. These large, heavy snakes average 5 ft. long and grow up to 7 ft. They are the most common constrictors, widely known as destroyers of rodents. Bull Snakes have a heavy nose plate, adapted for burrowing. All hiss very loudly when angered and will strike to defend themselves. But they tame down when captured (especially the western forms), and some make excellent pets. The Pine Snake is an eastern form of the Bull Snake, named for its favorite habitat—southern pine woods. It is relatively light-colored with large black patches on the back. Its food is small rabbits, squirrels, rats, and mice.

PINE SNAKE

**BULL SNAKE**

Farther west, the Bull Snake is more common. It is more yellowish than the Pine Snake and has a larger number of dark blotches. It often enters burrows to kill and feed on pocket gophers and ground squirrels. The Pacific Coast forms, known as Gopher Snakes are similar to the Bull Snake but smaller and with more blotches. All snakes in this group should be protected against wanton killing. There is no doubt of their value as one agent in rodent control.

Gopher

Bull

Pine

SCARLET KING SNAKE

RED KING SNAKE

COMMON KING SNAKE

**KING SNAKES** are a group of medium-sized snakes of normal proportions. They include some seven species, ranging from southern Canada through much of the U. S. All are constrictors and some are at least partially

immune to the poison of our venomous snakes. King Snakes feed on other snakes, but also eat many kinds of rodents. Red King or Milk Snake (30 in.) is a common eastern King Snake with red splotches bordered with black; the belly is pale, with black patches. It feeds mainly on rodents and not, as fables tell, by milking cows. Common King Snake is a shiny black with bands of yellow crossing in a chainlike pattern. It is larger (3½ to 4 ft.) than Red King Snake and is more common in open country. The small Scarlet King Snake (18 in.) may be confused with Coral Snake (p. 108), but note that each yellow band is bordered by black. California King Snake (3 ft.) is black with white bands; some have a white stripe down the back. Another midwestern form is peppered with yellow or white dots on most of its scales.

SPECKLED KING SNAKE

CALIFORNIA KING SNAKE

**Scarlet Snake**

**Coral Snake**

**Scarlet King Snake**

**SCARLET SNAKE,** unfortunately rare, is attractive and docile. It is a burrower, 16 to 24 in., occasionally found under rotting logs or on the ground at night. Its food appears to be small lizards and mice, which are killed by constriction. Eggs are laid. The markings have

much of the same pattern as on the Scarlet King Snake—yellow bands bordered by narrow black bands. But the bands do not encircle the belly. Coral Snake (p. 108) has black bands bordered by yellow.

Underside of Garter Snake Tail

Underside of Long-Nosed Snake Tail

**LONG-NOSED SNAKE** (2 to 3 ft.) does not have a long nose. Probably a burrower, it may be aided by its small, narrow head. Most have been caught at night. It is said to feed on lizards, snakes, and small mammals. Dark patches on the back are broken by bands of red, white, or yellow. Generally speckled, the color is variable; belly lighter with a few dark spots. This is the only harmless snake with a single row of scales under the tail.

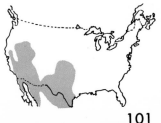

COMMON WATER SNAKE

PAINTED WATER SNAKE

**WATER SNAKES** are chiefly eastern species (nine) of lakes and rivers. They show little external adaptation to water life but are actually fine surface and underwater swimmers. They seek water when molested and there find their food, mainly fish and frogs. Heavily built, with short, narrow tails, they are harmless and should not be confused with the venomous southern Cottonmouth. However, Water Snakes are usually vicious; they do not tame or become good pets. The rear of the common Water Snake (30 in.) is crossbanded, with reddish-brown. Toward the head these

GREEN WATER SNAKE

DIAMOND-BACKED
WATER SNAKE

bands become large blotches. Diamond-backed Water
Snake is larger (3½ to 5 ft.) and darker. Its dark
blotches are reduced to diamonds over the backbone.
Painted Water Snake (3 to 5½ ft.) is dark above, with
a yellow or reddish belly. Green Water Snake (3 to
5½ ft.) is a dull olive green with a
vague, barred pattern. Color and
pattern are clearest in young
Water Snakes. All species get
darker as they grow older. As
many as 99 young are born alive.

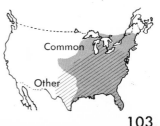

Common

Other

**PLAINS GARTER SNAKE**

**WESTERN GARTER SNAKE and Young**

**GARTER SNAKES** and their kin are perhaps more common and better known than any other snake. These 11 small (18 to 44 in.), striped species with keeled scales, related to Water Snakes, have similar habits. Like Water Snakes they eject an unpleasant fluid from vent glands when captured. Garter Snakes feed on frogs, toads, earthworms. Young are born alive in summer—20 or more at a time. Most Garter

Other Garter Snakes

Ribbon Snake

Snakes, fairly docile, do well in captivity. Common Garter Snake, more aggressive than others, is marked by three yellowish stripes; the dark area between is spotted. Some Garter Snakes have only two stripes. The center stripe of Plains Garter Snake is often a rich orange; the belly is darker than in common Garter Snake. The western species, with central stripe brighter than the side ones, is darker, but with light scales near the mouth. Ribbon Snake is thinner, smaller, with yellow or red stripes against brown scales. Its tail is nearly a third of the body length

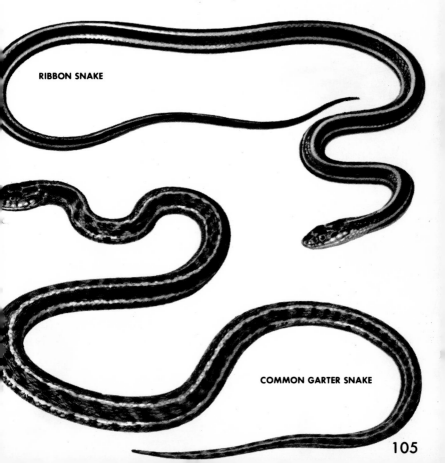

RIBBON SNAKE

COMMON GARTER SNAKE

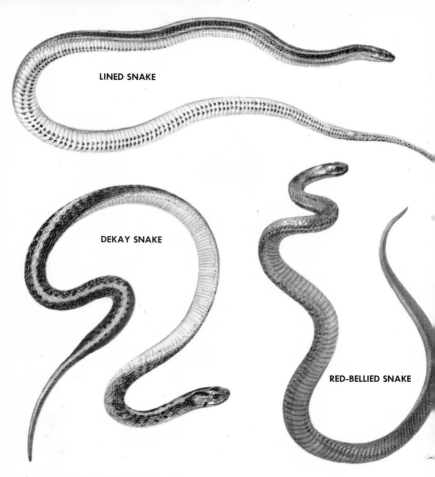

LINED SNAKE

DEKAY SNAKE

RED-BELLIED SNAKE

**SMALL STRIPED SNAKES** are common but inconspicuous. Lined Snake (12 to 20 in.) is a miniature Garter Snake with a yellow stripe down its back, black dots on the belly. The next two are related to Water Snakes. DeKay Snake (10 to 16 in.) is a brownish, secretive, burrowing species, common even near cities. The belly is yellow to pink, with black dots at sides. Red-bellied Snake (10 to 14 in.) is similar, but with red belly and yellow spots at back of head.

Red-bellied

Lined

DeKay

**FANGLESS NIGHT SNAKE**

**LYRE SNAKE**

**FANGLESS NIGHT SNAKE and LYRE SNAKE** are mildly poisonous. The former (15 in.) has enlarged teeth in the rear of its jaws, not true fangs. When it bites lizards, its saliva seems poisonous. Lyre Snake (3 ft.) is a rear-fanged poisonous snake (three species) with grooved fangs. Its poison seems harmless to man. The relatively large head and thin neck are characteristic of this snake. Lyre Snakes typically frequent rocky areas and feed on lizards.

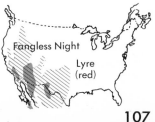

Fangless Night

Lyre (red)

**COMMON CORAL SNAKE**

**WESTERN CORAL SNAKE**

**CORAL SNAKES,** related to Cobras, are highly poisonous. Our two species have red, yellow, and black rings, the latter bordered by yellow. Common Coral Snake (30 to 39 in.) has black, yellow, and black from nose to back of head. Secretive and burrowing, it feeds mainly on lizards and other snakes. Western Coral Snake, smaller (18 in.), of limited range but similar habits, has black, yellow, and red successively on head and neck.

Western    Common

**COPPERHEAD**

**COTTONMOUTH**

**COPPERHEAD and COTTONMOUTH,** poisonous pit vipers, differ little from rattlers. Pits between eye and nostril, sensitive to heat, help them find and strike at warm-blooded prey. Copperheads (30 to 50 in.) are upland snakes, with coppery head and "hour glass" body patches. Cottonmouth or Water Moccasin (40 to 58 in.), larger, heavier, and more vicious, is a swamp snake feeding on fish and frogs. It is dark, not strongly marked. Both bear live young.

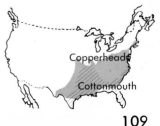

Copperhead

Cottonmouth

109

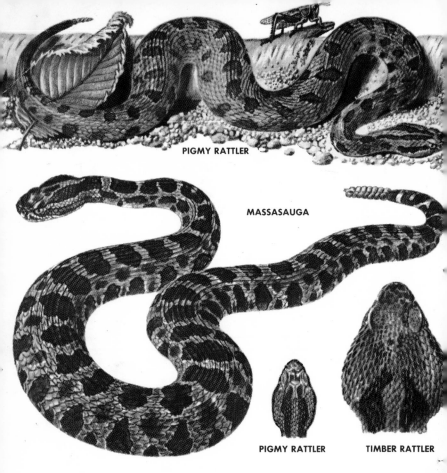

PIGMY RATTLER

MASSASAUGA

PIGMY RATTLER     TIMBER RATTLER

**MASSASAUGA and PIGMY RATTLERS,** very simi-lar to their larger relatives, do not have small scales on the top of the head. They are small, hence rela-tively less dangerous. The Massasauga (2 to 3½ ft.), a swamp Rattler, does not strike unless much annoyed.

Massasauga

Pigmy Rattler

The southern Pigmy Rattlers, also called Ground Rattlers, are smaller (18 to 24 in.) and prefer upland terrain. Though smaller, they are not mild-tempered, but rattle and strike when approached.

**Cross Section of Rattle**    **Button**    **Young**    **Older**    **Adult**    **Old Adult**

**RATTLESNAKES**    Rattlers (13 species) are typically American. Most kinds are found in the West, two in the East. Timber Rattler (3½ to 6 ft.) is a woodland species, yellowish with dark, V-shaped bands and dark tail. Eastern Diamondback, or Florida Rattler, named for the dorsal pattern, is our largest poisonous snake, averaging 5 ft. (record nearly 9 ft.). Westward is Prairie Rattler, varying in size (2½ to 5 ft.) and color, typically greenish yellow with darker blotches. Western Diamondback, or Texas Rattler, smaller (4½ to 7½ ft.), of rocky hillsides and open deserts, is brown with a lighter border, general color being gray. Red Rattler, similar to Texas, has reddish ground color. Strangest is Sidewinder (18 to 30 in.), with erect, horny scales over the eyes, strongly keeled scales, and a rapid, sidewise motion over sand. The Rattler's rattle, a horny structure, gains a segment each time the snake sheds; it helps tell age. Rattlers are nervous, aggressive, live poorly in captivity. Food: rabbits, gophers, rats, mice, other small mammals. Young are born alive; litters of 12 are common.

Prairie Rattler

Timber Rattler

Sidewinder

Red    Western    Eastern

111

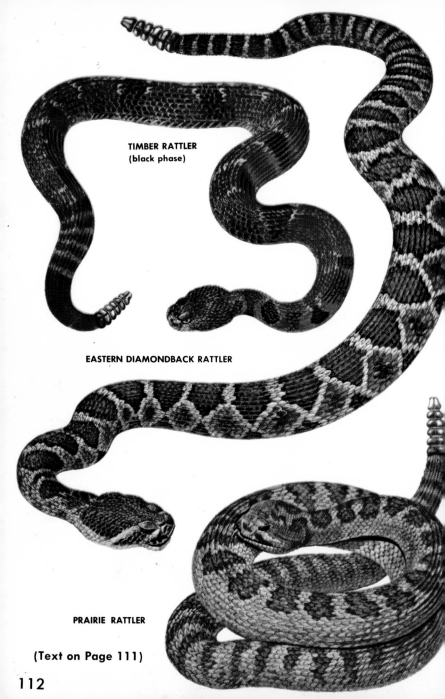

TIMBER RATTLER
(black phase)

EASTERN DIAMONDBACK RATTLER

PRAIRIE RATTLER

(Text on Page 111)

SIDEWINDER

WESTERN DIAMONDBACK
RATTLER

RED RATTLER

(Text on Page 111)

113

**ALLIGATOR**

Nest

Alligator Hatching

Young Alligator

**ALLIGATORS** and **CROCODILES** form a distinct group of reptiles of ancient lineage. Once common in southern swamps, alligators have been reduced in number and range by hunters. Large specimens, 10 ft. and over, are now rare. They are not especially long-lived; a 10-footer is 20 or 25 years old. Alligators are not usually dangerous. Reports of "man-eaters" usually refer to crocodiles of Africa or southern Asia. Young alligators, hard to feed, do not make good pets. American Crocodile is smaller, thinner, more agile than

CROCODILE

the alligator; its snout is pointed, narrower. Some of the teeth protrude, bulldog-fashion, from the sides of its jaw. Alligators and crocodiles feed on fish, turtles, birds, crayfish, crabs, and other water life. Both lay eggs, hatched by heat of the sun and of decaying vegetation. Crocodiles prefer salt marshes and even swim out into the ocean. Alligators prefer fresh water. Both alligators and crocodiles are now protected by law.

Alligator

Crocodile

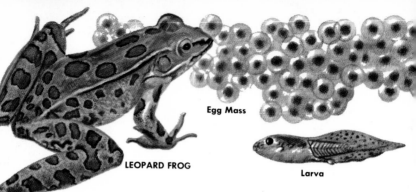

Egg Mass

LEOPARD FROG

Larva

**AMPHIBIANS** were the animals which, eons ago, first ventured out of water to live on land. Those that survive today are still poorly adapted to terrestial life. Most spend at least part of their lives in water or in moist surroundings. Amphibians vary considerably in appearance, but all differ from reptiles in never having clawed feet or true scaly skins. Of three groups, two are common. The salamanders and their kin are tailed amphibians. The frogs and toads are tailless when mature and often have hind legs better developed.

Amphibians lay jelly-covered eggs singly, in clumps, or in strings in quiet water or on moist leaf mold. These eggs hatch into larvae or tadpoles, which usually breathe by means of gills and spend much or all of their life in water. Tadpoles feed on microscopic plants and have mouth and digestive parts adapted for this diet. Larvae become air-breathing adults which may live in water, or which later return to the water to mate and lay eggs. Adults feed largely on insects. In the

Lizard Forefoot

Frog Forefoot

Salamander Forefoot

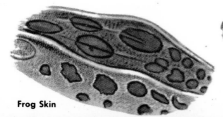

Egg Mass

Larva

TIGER
SALAMANDER

North they hibernate during winter underground or in mud at the bottom of ponds.

Frogs are divided into five major groups, as illustrated on page 6. The Tailed Toads (p. 120) represent the first. The Fire-bellied Toads occur in Mexico and South America. The Spadefoots (p. 121) are the next group, followed by a large diverse group (pp. 122-131) which includes toads, Tree Frogs, and Chorus, Robber, and Whistling Frogs. True Frogs and Narrow-mouthed Frogs (pp. 132-136) belong to the last group, which is almost as large as the toad group.

The five major groups of salamanders are redivided into eight families, of which seven occur in the United States. The group represented by the Slimy Salamanders and newts includes by far the largest number of species. The Tiger Salamanders and kin (pp. 144-145) are the only others that spend time on land. The Caecilians—tropical, burrowing species—are living fossils, more closely related to salamanders than to frogs.

Frog Skin

Lizard Skin

**Toad Calling**

**Toad Extends Tongue**

1

2

**Toad Catches Fly**

**FROGS and TOADS** cannot be clearly distinguished, though toads usually have rough or warty skins and live mainly on land. Frogs have smoother skins and live in water or wet places. Toads are plump, broad, and less streamlined than frogs. They are slower and cannot jump as well. Their eyes are larger, too. Some frogs have such varied markings that identification is difficult. Added to this, the skin color and markings of some species change with their surroundings. Most male frogs and toads can inflate a sac in their throat when they make their characteristic sounds. There are about 99 species and subspecies of tailless amphibians in this country. These fit into seven families, the largest of which are the tree frogs, the true toads, and the frogs.

**Skin Color Changes with Surroundings**

**TADPOLES** are the immature or larval stage of frogs and toads. The Robber Frogs (p. 130) are the only native frogs which do not have free-swimming tadpoles. Tadpoles are difficult to identify. The pictures may help you name some species. (See p. 133 for the Bullfrog tadpole.) Collect frogs' eggs or small tadpoles along the shores of ponds and ditches in spring; place them in an aquarium containing pond water and water plants. Do not overstock. As tadpoles hatch and begin to grow they will feed off bits of lettuce, which partly rots in the water. As your tadpoles change into frogs, provide a wooden float on which they can climb and rest.

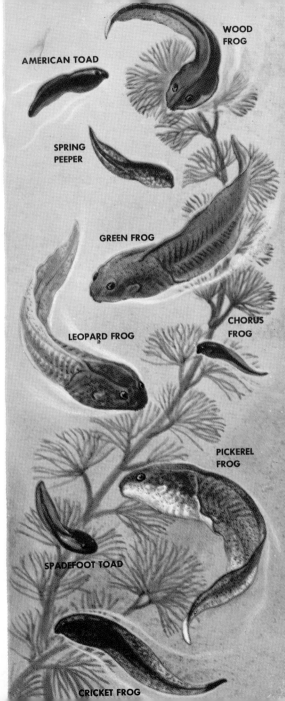

AMERICAN TOAD

WOOD FROG

SPRING PEEPER

GREEN FROG

LEOPARD FROG

CHORUS FROG

PICKEREL FROG

SPADEFOOT TOAD

CRICKET FROG

Female

Male

**TAILED or BELL TOAD** is primitive. The male has a distinct "tail." After breeding in late spring or early summer, strings of large eggs are found attached to rocks in mountain streams. Tadpoles cling to the rocks by means of a large sucking disc around the mouth.

These small toads, 1 to 2 in. long, vary greatly in color, from gray and black to pink and brown. Note the webbed feet and the short, wide head with a light line sometimes across it.

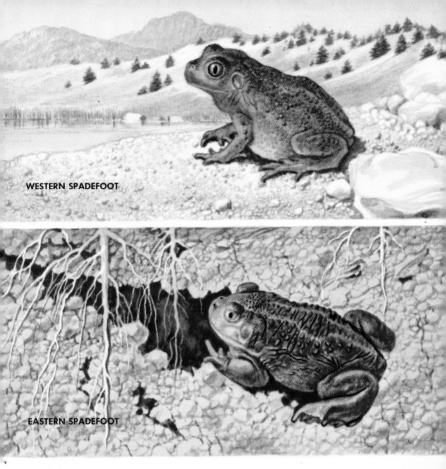

WESTERN SPADEFOOT

EASTERN SPADEFOOT

**SPADEFOOT TOADS** (four species) have fleshy, webbed feet with large, horny, spade-like warts. In burrowing, the toad corkscrews backward and downward into the soil. It is found under logs or rocks, in shallow holes, coming out at night or after heavy rains to feed. Medium-sized (1 ½ to 3 in. long), it has relatively smooth skin. Eyes are large, with vertical pupils. Breeding is in late spring and early summer. Eggs are attached to plants at the water's edge.

121

AMERICAN TOAD

**TOADS,** a much-maligned group of amphibians, were once credited with causing warts. Though clumsy, they are well adapted to life on land, feeding mainly on insects and slugs. They protect themselves by burrowing playing dead, inflating their bodies, and exuding through their skin a white fluid which, in contact with eyes or mouth, is very poisonous. In breeding season and especially when it is raining, males make a very characteristic trilling call. Toads tame easily and make unusual pets; feed them mealworms.

American

Fowler's

FOWLER'S TOAD

The American Toad (13 species in U.S.) is the common eastern species, 2 to 4 in. long. Males have a darker throat. Fowler's Toad (the eastern race of Woodhouse Toads) is more greenish and smaller, usually with smaller, more numerous warts and with a white line down the back. The Western Toad (2 to 5 in.) is very warty; the belly is mottled and the head more pointed than in eastern toads. The Great Plains Toad, common along irrigation ditches and streams, is gray or brownish and somewhat varied in pattern.

Western

Great Plains

GREAT PLAINS TOAD

123

**CHORUS FROGS** are seven species of small amphibians usually less than 2 in. long. They are locally called Tree Frogs (though they rarely climb) and Cricket Frogs —names which cause confusion. All Chorus Frogs have slender bodies and pointed snouts. They breed early in spring, attaching small masses of eggs to leaves and stems in water. They are common at this time but later seem to disappear entirely, so their habits are not well known. They seldom climb more than a few inches above the ground; some cannot climb at all. The Striped Chorus Frogs are small ($3/4$ to $1 1/2$ in.), brownish or olive-colored, with distinct dark stripes on

STRIPED CHORUS FROG

ORNATE CHORUS FROG

the back. The closely related Swamp Chorus Frog is common in southern ditches and swamps. It is slender, olive green, with an even, granular skin. Spots on the back are irregular. The Ornate Chorus Frog, a small edition of the Wood Frog (p. 135), completely lacks toe pads. It is chestnut brown with a dark mask and with dark spots on the sides; length 1 to 1¼ in. Strecker Chorus Frog, found farther west, is a more stocky species (1 to ¾ in.), usually gray or greenish with darker spots and blotches on back and limbs.

STRECKER CHORUS FROG

**COMMON TREE FROG**

**GREEN TREE FROG**

**CANYON TREE FROG**

**PINE TREE FROG**

(Text on Page 128)

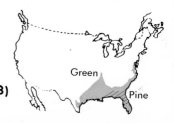

126

**SQUIRREL TREE FROG**

**PACIFIC TREE FROG**

**SPRING PEEPER**

**WHISTLING TREE FROG**

**(Text on Page 128)**

127

**TREE FROGS or HYLAS,** a large family of amphibians, are related to the toads but smaller (most are ¾ to 2 in.). Lightly built, they live in trees and shrubs, clinging with the sticky pads on their toes. The skin, often slightly warty or rough, is usually brown or greenish. The call, heard in early spring, is loud, clear, musical. The frogs vary much in color and pattern, and can to a degree change color with their surroundings.

Common Tree Frog, with orange or brown thighs, back spotted or mottled gray or brown, skin slightly rough, is heard in midsummer in woods near water. Green Tree Frog, most attractive, 1½ to 2½ in., with smooth green skin, slender and long-legged, has a penetrating honking call. Canyon Tree Frog can change its color from brown or black to pale pinkish gray. The skin is rough. Eggs are laid singly, in water. Pine Tree Frog, legs brownish with small orange spots, irregular cross on back, ranges from greenish gray to reddish brown; found only in pine woods. Squirrel Tree Frog, green to brown, usually spotted, skin smooth, has light stripe from eye to forelegs. Pacific Tree Frog is gray, brown, or green; attractive; back sometimes spotted; brown V between eyes; 1 to 2 in. Spring Peeper, best-known eastern Tree Frog, ¾ to 1¼ in., common in woodland swamps, is light brown or gray with dark diagonal cross on back. Whistling Tree Frog, dusky-colored, with greenish thigh and three rows of spots or a cross on back, utters a unique whistle.

**SPRING PEEPER**

**CRICKET FROGS** are really small (¾ to 1½ in.) tree frogs without toe pads. Hence they cannot climb. Color varies from brown to gray and green, with darker markings that may be brown or even reddish. A dark triangle is usually present atop the head. The skin is slightly rough. Cricket Frogs, common throughout the East, get their name from their call—a sharp, rapid metallic clicking. Eggs are laid singly, attached to plants in ponds and pools. Two species.

TEXAS ROBBER FROG

**ROBBER FROGS,** sometimes called Barking Frogs, are West Indian species, introduced and becoming common in the South, along the Gulf and in Florida. Our single native species lives in limestone ledges or caves. Eggs are laid in moisture-filled crevices. The tadpoles do not hatch but remain within the egg till they have developed into tiny frogs. Robber Frogs are short, squat, with wide, flat heads. The tiny Florida species is only ⅗ to 1⅕ in. long. The larger Texas species (2 to 3½ in.) has a call like a barking dog. All three species are usually dark in color.

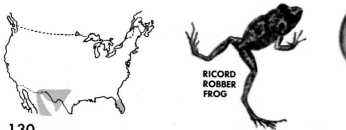

RICORD ROBBER FROG

Tadpole in Egg (magnified 3 times)

WHITE-LIPPED FROG

WHISTLING FROG

**WHITE-LIPPED and WHISTLING FROGS** are really Mexican species. The first is a medium-sized, smooth-skinned frog (1½ to 2 in.), marked as its name indicates. It lays eggs in a frothy mass at the edge of ponds. Whistling Frog (two species) is smaller, with more pointed nose and granular skin. Its eggs, laid on land, hatch into legged frogs. There are no free-swimming tadpoles. This dull gray-green frog makes a faint whistling chirp.

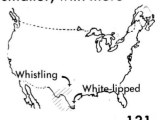

Whistling

White-lipped

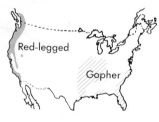

**GOPHER FROG**

**GOPHER and RED-LEGGED FROGS** introduce the "true" frog group—16 common species that have smooth, narrow bodies and long hind legs. The Gopher Frog (2½ to 4½ in.), gray with small black spots, lives in the burrows of Gopher Turtles or crayfish. Though fairly common, they are rarely seen. The large Red-legged Frog of the West (2 to 5 in.) is an even dark brown or olive above, and colored below as its name indicates. It is a frog of moist forests, breeding in June or July.

Red-legged

Gopher

**RED-LEGGED FROG**

GREEN FROG (female)

BULLFROG (male)

## BULLFROG and GREEN FROG
The Bullfrog is largest of our frogs (4 to 7½ in.). The male has very large "ears" (tympani) behind the eyes; the female's ears are smaller. The color is usually drab green. In the North, the large tadpole does not mature till the second year. The Green Frog is smaller (2 to 4 in.), with a yellowish throat, especially in the males. Both of these common frogs live in ponds and swamps. Both are solitary, laying eggs in spreading surface masses.

Bull

Green

BULLFROG Tadpole

133

PICKEREL FROG        LEOPARD FROG

**PICKEREL and LEOPARD FROGS** are common, attractive, and sometimes confusing. The former has square or rectangular spots on the back and reddish sides; legs are orange or reddish. Leopard or Meadow Frog has more rounded spots and greenish sides; legs

Leopard

Pickerel

are greenish. It also has a pair of light lines running from the eye back along the sides. Both frogs are slender, smooth-skinned, and about 2 to 4 in. long. Both are often found in moist, grassy meadows.

134

**WOOD FROG**

**WOOD and SPOTTED FROGS** The first is one of the most attractive common frogs: its fawn-brown skin is set off by a dark mask over the eyes. It prefers moist woods, breeds from May to July in woodland pools. Eggs are laid near shore in rounded mass, 2 to 4 in. across, containing 2000 to 3000 individual eggs. Length: 1½ to 3 in. The Spotted Frog (3 to 4 in.) is a western species typical of mountain areas. It is dark brown, sometimes spotted with skin slightly roughened. A light streak marks the edge of the upper jaw.

**SPOTTED FROG**

135

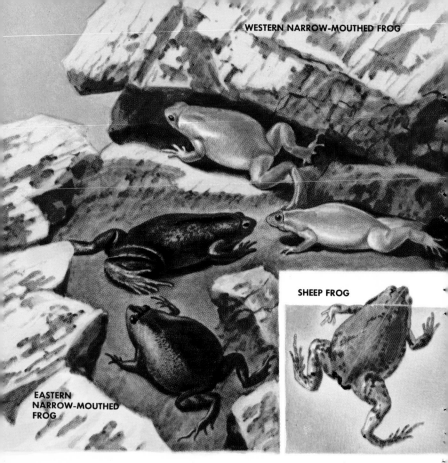

WESTERN NARROW-MOUTHED FROG

SHEEP FROG

EASTERN NARROW-MOUTHED FROG

**NARROW-MOUTHED FROGS** have small, wedge-shaped heads with a fold of skin crossing the head just back of the eyes. They are dark or mottled; undersides lighter. Nocturnal frogs with tiny voices, they often hide under logs and rocks. The Sheep Frog, a related species, has narrow head but loose, dark skin, with a narrow yellow or orange stripe down the back. It breeds (March-September) in shallow ponds or large rain-water pools.

Narrow-mouthed

Sheep

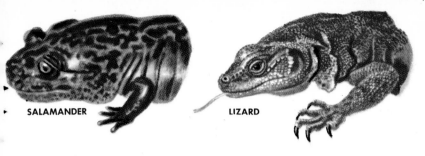

SALAMANDER          LIZARD

**SALAMANDERS** are tailed amphibians. About 135 kinds, in seven families, are found in this country. They differ from lizards (pp. 44-45) in lacking a scaly skin and claws. Salamanders never have more than four toes on the front feet; lizards usually have five. Many salamanders are nocturnal; all avoid direct sun. During the breeding season they move about more and hence are more likely to be seen. Some spend their entire lives in water; others live on moist land, returning to water only to mate and lay eggs. The eggs, with a jelly-like coating, are laid singly or in small clumps. Some terrestrial salamanders have no larval stage. Salamanders may be kept in terraria like frogs and toads. Feed them mealworms or other live insects. Most species are too small and unattractive for pets.

Eggs of
Hellbender

Eggs of
Four-toed Salamander

Eggs of
Spotted Salamander

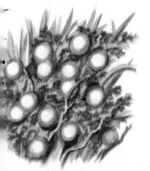

**MUDPUPPY or WATERDOG** (12 in.) is a large aquatic salamander of rivers and lakes. The color varies —often dark brown above, paler on belly with dark spots. A larva throughout life, it has bushy red gills. Eggs are laid in late spring attached to rocks under water. The eggs hatch in 40 to 60 days. Hatchlings, striped on their back and sides, are about an inch long; they mature in about five years. Three species occur in the United States.

CONGO-EEL

**CONGO-EEL and HELLBENDER** are large aquatic salamanders. The former (two species), smooth and eel-like, grows 30 to 36 in. long, with four tiny, useless, one- to three-toed feet. It is often found in ditches, in burrows, or under debris. The female lays a mass of eggs under mud or rotted leaves. She may remain near to guard them. The Hellbender (16 to 20 in.) is shorter and broader, and lives farther north. Its wrinkled skin makes identification easy. The color varies from spotted yellowish to red and brown. Eggs are laid under rocks in shallow water.

Hellbender

Congo-eel

HELLBENDER

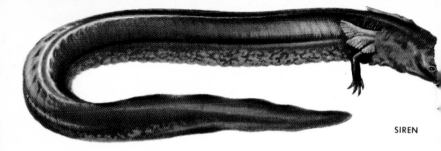

SIREN

**SIRENS and MUD SIRENS** are southern salamanders of rivers, swamps, and ponds. Both have external gills and both have only front legs. The Sirens are larger (about 30 in.), gray, olive green or blackish with spots and blotches. The Mud Sirens (two species), 5 to 8 in. long, have smaller gills and legs. They occur in southern streams and waterways. Light stripes down the back and sides are a characteristic marking. Both feed on insects, worms, larvae, and other small water animals.

Siren

Mud Siren

MUD SIREN

GIANT SALAMANDER

OLYMPIC SALAMANDER

**GIANT and OLYMPIC SALAMANDERS** are two northwestern species. The first, the largest western salamander (9 to 12 in.), is our largest land species. It is found on moist slopes under rocks and logs. Larvae live in nearby streams. The back color varies—usually mottled; legs darker. Olympic Salamander, smaller (3½ in.), prefers the humid coastal coniferous forests, where it is usually found in or along clear streams.

Olympic
Giant
(red)

141

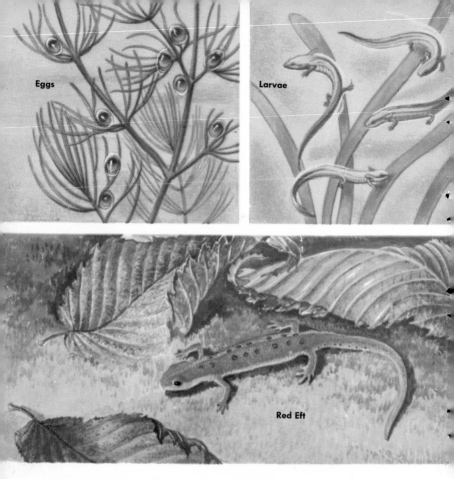

Eggs

Larvae

Red Eft

**NEWTS** are attractive, interesting salamanders. Of the five species, the eastern (3 in. long) is perhaps the best known. Its eggs, laid in spring, on stems and leaves of water plants, hatch into larvae. After 3 or 4 months in the water these usually leave to spend 2 or 3 years on land as an unusual form, known as the Red Eft. When the Efts return permanently to water, they change color and develop a broad swimming tail. Some newts skip the eft stage. Newts feed on worms, insect larvae and small aquatic animals. They are per-

EASTERN NEWT—Adults

WESTERN NEWT

haps the best salamanders to keep as pets. Red Efts, fed on live insects, do well in terraria. Adults thrive in aquaria, feeding on small bits of liver or other meat. The Western Newt is about twice the size of the eastern species and differs in appearance too. Adults are land-dwellers, returning to water only to breed. They are reddish or dark brown, belly much lighter yellow or orange. Found in moist woods and mountain ponds.

Western

Eastern

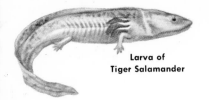

Larva of
Tiger Salamander

**SPOTTED SALAMANDER** (7 in.) has large, round, yellow, or orange spots on a black skin. Like others in this group (11 species) it has vertical grooves on its sides. It is found in moist woods; breeds in ponds and temporary pools. Adults migrate considerably, returning to water to breed. They feed on worms, grubs, and insects.

**TIGER SALAMANDER** (8 in.) is like the Spotted, but the spots, when present, are larger, more irregular, and extend down the sides and onto the belly. Some larvae do not develop into the land form; they spend their entire life in water, where they eventually breed. Tiger Salamanders are known to live over 10 years.

**MARBLED SALAMANDER** (4 in.) is smaller than others in this group, but like most is a stout, thick-set creature. Variable markings on the black skin, white on males, grayish on females, in irregular fused bands. The larvae are a mottled brown.

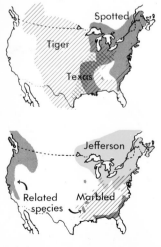

Spotted

Tiger

Texas

Jefferson

Related species

Marbled

**JEFFERSON SALAMANDER** is slender (6½ in.); also called Blue-spotted, for the markings on its brownish skin. It lives in woods along swamps and streams. Trunk and tail have vertical grooves.

**TEXAS SALAMANDER** (5½ in.) is found in varying habitats from swampy lowlands to upland woods. It is a burrower beneath logs and rocks near streams. The color is a faintly blotched slate gray or brown, lighter beneath.

SPOTTED SALAMANDER

TIGER SALAMANDER

MARBLED SALAMANDER

JEFFERSON SALAMANDER

TEXAS SALAMANDER

145

COMMON
DUSKY
SALAMANDER

ALLEGHENY
DUSKY
SALAMANDER

**DUSKY SALAMANDERS** comprise nine species of
average-sized (3½ in.), inconspicuous salamanders with
highly variable color and pattern. Their dark, mottled
skins blend with rocks and moss along streams where
they live. The sides are grooved vertically. Note a small

light bar from eye to jaw. The Allegheny Mountain and Shovel-nosed
species differ from the common eastern in having a light, irregularly
spotted band down the back.

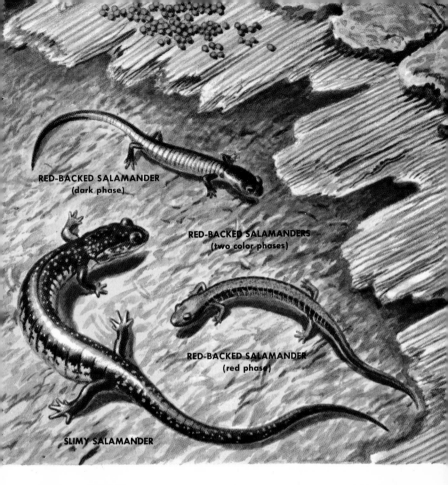

RED-BACKED SALAMANDER
(dark phase)

RED-BACKED SALAMANDERS
(two color phases)

RED-BACKED SALAMANDER
(red phase)

SLIMY SALAMANDER

**RED-BACKED and SLIMY SALAMANDERS** are land species of our largest group (19 species). Often found in leaf mold and under rotted logs, both breed on land and lay eggs in moist nests in rotted bark or logs. Red-backed (3 in. long) has two color phases; only one has the red stripe down the back. Slimy Salamander, larger (6 in.), has blue-black skin with small, irregular light spots on back, and grayish belly.

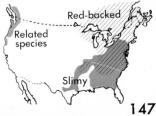

Red-backed

Related species

Slimy

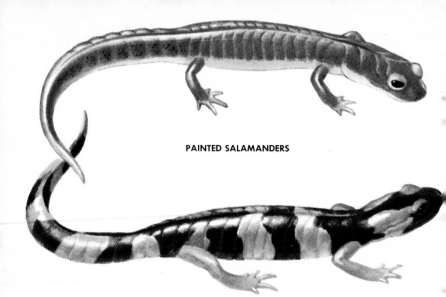

PAINTED SALAMANDERS

**PAINTED and WORM SALAMANDERS** are western species. The single species of Painted varies from black to red, usually with red or yellow orange blotches. These medium-sized salamanders (4 to 5 in.) occur in the mountains, in oak and evergreen forests. They exhibit an unusual and complex courtship pattern. The Worm Salamander (4 in.) is, as its name implies, thin and wormlike, with a very long tail. The color is dark, often spotted or streaked. The salamander is found under rotted logs or leaves where it lays its eggs, from which tiny miniatures of the adults emerge.

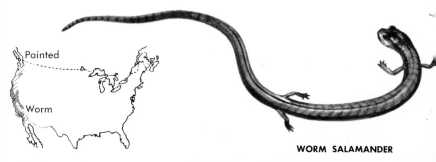

Painted

Worm

WORM SALAMANDER

**GREEN and TREE SALAMANDERS,** 4 in. long (five species), live on opposite sides of the country. Green Salamander is found on the rocky hillsides of the Appalachians, under logs or in crevices of rocks. It is dark, with greenish blotches. The Tree Salamander of the Pacific Coast frequently lives in water-soaked cavities of trees. Sometimes a whole colony is found in one of these holes, where eggs are laid, also. Tree Salamanders also live on the ground, under logs, rocks, and bark. Their color is light brown, paler below with few if any markings.

GREEN SALAMANDER

Green

Tree

149

OZARK BLIND SALAMANDER

TEXAS BLIND SALAMANDER

**BLIND SALAMANDERS** are unusual animals found only in deep wells and underground streams of caves. They are a pale yellowish in color, with eyes reduced in size or completely undeveloped. The larvae of the Ozark Blind Salamander (adults 3¾ in.), found in open

Ozark

Georgia

Texas

streams, have dark-colored skins and normal eyes. The young of the Texas species (adults 4 in.) resemble the pale adults. Another rare Blind Salamander has been found in Georgia.

RED SALAMANDER

PURPLE SALAMANDER

RED SALAMANDER
(young)

**PURPLE and RED SALAMANDERS** often belie their names. The Purple (5 in. long; three species) is actually brownish or reddish brown, with vague spots or blotches. Young adults, newly transformed from larvae, are brighter red. This is also true of the Red Salamander (5 in.; two species). Young adults are bright red with small dark spots; older ones, dull and darker. Both of these salamanders are commonest in hilly or mountain areas along streams or near ponds.

Purple

Red

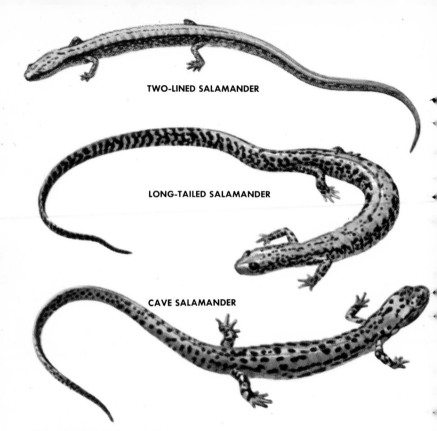

**TWO-LINED SALAMANDER**

**LONG-TAILED SALAMANDER**

**CAVE SALAMANDER**

# TWO-LINED, LONG-TAILED and CAVE SALA-MANDERS represent a common but inconspicuous group (eight species). Two-lined (3 in.) is so marked, with a broken row of dark dots between the lines on its sides. Long-tailed (about 5 in.) is thin, yellow to orange, mottled or spotted. Both prefer moist sites under logs and rocks, though the Two-lined also prefers brook-

sides. The Cave Salamander (5 in.) is seen near the entrances of caves and under moist, overhanging rocks. Color is variable, usually yellow to orange with scattered black spots.

**FOUR-TOED SALAMANDER** is so called because both front and hind feet are four-toed. It is one of the smallest salamanders (2½ in.), fairly common in wooded areas, swamps, and bogs. The dull red-brown back is mottled with darker patches; the belly is lighter, with brown spots. Males are smaller than females and have longer tails. The female lays her eggs in a mossy cavity and stays with them till they hatch, in about two months. The larvae leave the water in six weeks to complete their development on land. They mature in about two years.

Four-toed

Margined

Dwarf
Four-toed

# BOOKS FOR FURTHER STUDY

Bishop, Sherman C., HANDBOOK OF SALAMANDERS, Comstock Pub. Co., Ithaca, N.Y., 1947. An excellent reference and a companion to the volumes by Carr and Smith, listed below.

Carr, Archie, HANDBOOK OF TURTLES, Comstock Pub. Co., Ithaca, N.Y., 1952. The best and most complete guide to American turtles, with ample data on life histories and identification.

Ditmars, Raymond, REPTILES OF NORTH AMERICA, Doubleday and Co., Garden City, N.Y., 1949. A general, non-technical reference to the major North American species. Illustrated with photographs.

Pope, Clifford H., SNAKES ALIVE AND HOW THEY LIVE, Viking Press, New York, 1937. A very readable account of snakes and their habits, by a top authority.

Schmidt, Karl P., and Davis, D. D., FIELD BOOK OF SNAKES OF THE U.S. AND CANADA, G. P. Putnam's Sons, New York, 1941. A compact, detailed guide to identification of species and subspecies. Of special value to the more advanced amateur.

Smith, Hobart M., HANDBOOK OF LIZARDS, Comstock Pub. Co., Ithaca, N.Y., 1946. A definitive reference to the most common reptiles, with full information on identification and how they live.

Wright, A., and Wright, A., A HANDBOOK OF FROGS AND TOADS, Comstock Pub. Co., Ithaca, N.Y., 1949. An excellent, detailed field guide to these amphibians; non-technical and well illustrated.

## ZOOS, MUSEUMS, AND STUDY COLLECTIONS

Here are some well-known places where reptiles and amphibians can be studied alive or as part of permanent exhibits or collections:

Washington, D. C.: U.S. National Museum, National Zoological Park

New York City: American Museum of Natural History, Staten Island Zoo, Bronx Park Zoo

Chicago, Ill.: Natural History Museum, Brookfield Zoo, Lincoln Park Zoo

Boston, Mass.: Harvard Museum of Comparative Zoology

Philadelphia, Pa.: Philadelphia Zoological Park

Los Angeles, Calif.: Los Angeles County Museum

Ann Arbor, Mich.: Univ. of Mich. Museum of Zoology

San Antonio, Texas: San Antonio Zoo

San Diego, Calif.: Zoological Park

Silver Springs, Fla.: Ross Allen's Reptile Institute

Miami, Fla.: Serpentarium.

Berkeley, Calif.: Univ. of Calif. Mus. of Vert. Zoology

# SCIENTIFIC NAMES

Following are the scientific names of species illustrated in this book. Heavy type indicates pages where species appear. The genus name is first, then the species. If the genus name is abbreviated, it is the same as the genus name mentioned just before it.

**20** Leatherback: Dermochelys coriacea.
Hawksbill: Eretmochelys imbricata.

**21** Loggerhead: Caretta caretta.
Green: Chelonia mydas.

**22** Sternotherus odoratus.

**23** Common: Kinosternon subrubrum subrubrum.
Yellow-necked: K. flavescens.

**24** Chelydra serpentina.

**25** Macroclemys temmincki.

**26** Amyda ferox.

**27** Gopherus polyphemus.

**28-29** Pseudemys scripta elegans.

**30** Pseudemys floridana hieroglyphica.

**31** Deirochelys reticularia.

**32** Eastern: Chrysemys picta picta.
Mississippi: C. picta dorsalis.
Western: C. picta belli.

**33** Chrysemys picta marginata.

**34** Graptemys pseudogeographica kohni.

**35** Graptemys geographica.

**36** Emydoidea blandingi.

**37** Malaclemys terrapin.

**38** Eastern: Terrapene carolina.
Western: T. ornata.

**40** Clemmys guttata.

**41** Clemmys marmorata.

**42** Clemmys muhlenbergi.

**43** Clemmys insculpta.

**46** Tubercular: Phyllodactylus tuberculatus.
Least: Sphaerodactylus cinereus.
Turkish: Hemidactylus turcicus.

**47** Coleonyx variegatus.

**48** Anole: Anolis carolinensis.
Chameleon: Chameleo vulgaris.

**49** Sauromalus obesus.

**50** Dipsosaurus dorsalis.

**51** True: Iguana iguana rhinolopha (juv.)
Spiny: Ctenosaura pectinata (juv.)

**52** Crotaphytus collaris.

**53** Gambelia wislizeni.

**54** Climbing: Urosaurus ornatus.
Ground: Uta stansburiana.

**55** Earless: Holbrookia maculata.
Zebra-tailed: Callisaurus draconoides.
Fringe-footed: Uma notata.

**56** Texas Spiny: Sceloporus olivaceus.
Western Fence: S. occidentalis.
Ground: S. graciosus.
Desert Scaly: S. poinsetti.
Desert Spiny: S. magister.

**57** Sceloporus undulatus.

**58** Desert: Phrynosoma platyrhinos.
Short-horned: P. douglassi.

**59** Phrynosoma cornutum.

**60** Granite: Xantusia henshawi.
Arizona: X. arizonae.

**61** Eumeces obsoletus.

**62** Gr. Five-lined: Eumeces laticeps.
Common Western: E. skiltonianus.
Greater Western: E. gilberti.
Sonoran: E. obsoletus.

**63** Eumeces fasciatus.

**64** Brown: Scincella laterale.
Sand: Neoseps reynoldsi.

**65** Six-lined: Cnemidophorus sexlineatus.
Tiger: C. tigris.

**66** Texas: Gerrhonotus liocephalus.
Western: Elgaria multicarinatus.

**67** Ophisaurus ventralis.

**68** Worm: Rhineura floridana.
Footless: Anniella pulchra.

**69** Heloderma suspectum.

**72** Leptotyphlops.

**73** Rubber: Charina bottae.
Rosy: Lichanura roseofusca.

**74** Abastor erythrogrammus.

**75** Farancia abacura.

**76** Eastern: Diadophis punctatus.
Western: D. amabilis.

**77** Keeled: Opheodrys aestivus.
Smooth-scaled: O. vernalis.

**78** Cone-nosed: Virginia striatula.
Ground: Sonora semiannulata.
Short-tailed: Stilosoma extenuatum.
Shovel-nosed: Chionactis occipitalis.

**79** Black Swamp: Seminatrix pygaea.
Striped Swamp: Liodytes alleni.
Sharp-tailed: Contia tenuis.
Sand: Chilomeniscus cinctus.

**80** Chilomeniscus cinctus.

**81** Western: Heterodon nasicus.
Common: H. platyrhinos.

**82** Vine: Oxybelis aeneus.
Western Hook-nosed: Gyalopion canum.
Fanged Night: Leptodeira annulata septentrionalis.

**83** Flat-headed: Tantilla coronata.
Yellow-lipped: Rhadinaea flavilata.
Texas Hook-nosed: Ficimia streckeri.
Worm: Carphophis amoena.
Black-striped: Coniophanes imperialis.

**85** Eastern: Coluber constrictor constrictor.
Western: C. constrictor mormon.

**86** Masticophis flagellum flagellum.

**87** Masticophis taeniatus taeniatus.

**88** Salvadora lineata.

**89** Phyllorhynchus browni.

**90** Gray: Elaphe obsoleta spiloides.
Yellow: E. obsoleta quadrivittata.

**91** Elaphe obsoleta obsoleta.

**92** Elaphe guttata guttata.

**93** Elaphe vulpina.

**94** Drymarchon corais.

**95** Arizona elegans.

**96** Pituophis melanoleucus melanoleucus.

**97** Pituophis melanoleucus sayi.

**98** Scarlet: Lampropeltis triangulum elapsoides.
Red: L. triangulum triangulum.
Common: L. getulus getulus.

**99** Speckled: Lampropeltis getulus holbrooki.
Calif.: L. getulus californiae.

**100** Cemophora doliata.

**101** Rhinocheilus lecontei.

**102** Common: Natrix sipedon sipedon.
Painted: N. erythrogaster erythrogaster.

**103** Green: Natrix cyclopion.
Diamond-backed: N. rhombifera.

**104** Plains: Thamnophis radix.
Western: T. elegans.

**105** Ribbon: Thamnophis sauritus.
Common: T. ordinatus.

**106** Lined: Tropidoclonion lineatum.
DeKay: Storeria dekayi.
Red-bellied: S. occipitomaculata.

**107** Fangless Night: Hypsiglena ochrorhyncha.
Lyre: Trimorphodon lambda.

**108** Common: Micrurus fulvius.
Western: Micruroides euryxanthus.

**109** Copperhead: Agkistrodon contortrix.
Cottonmouth: A. piscivorus.

**110** Pigmy: Sistrurus miliarius.
Massasauga: S. catenatus.

**112** Timber: Crotalus horridus.
Eastern Diamondback: C. adamanteus.
Prairie: C. viridis.

**113** Sidewinder: Crotalus cerastes.
Western Diamondback: C. atrox.
Red: C. ruber.
**114** Alligator mississippiensis.
**115** Crocodilus acutus.
**118** Bufo americanus.
**120** Ascaphus truei.
**121** Western: Spea hammondi.
Eastern: Scaphiopus holbrooki.
**122** American: Bufo americanus.
Fowler's: B. woodhousei fowleri.
**123** Western: Bufo boreas.
Great Plains: B. cognatus.
**124** Swamp: Pseudacris nigrita nigrita.
Striped: P. nigrita triseriata.
**125** Ornate: Pseudacris ornata.
Strecker: P. streckeri.
**126** Common: Hyla versicolor.
Green: H. cinerea.
Canyon: H. arenicolor.
Pine: H. femoralis.
**127** Squirrel: Hyla squirella.
Pacific: H. regilla.
Spring Peeper: H. crucifer.
Whistling: H. avivoca.
**129** Acris crepitans.
**130** Texas: Eleutherodactylus latrans.
Ricord: E. ricordi planirostris.
**131** White-lipped: Leptodactylus labialis.
Whistling: Syrrhophus marnocki.
**132** Gopher: Rana areolata.
Red-legged: R. aurora.
**133** Green: Rana clamitans.
Bullfrog: R. catesbeiana.
**134** Pickerel: Rana palustris.
Leopard: R. pipiens.
**135** Wood: Rana sylvatica.
Spotted: R. pretiosa.
**136** Western: Microhyla olivacea.
Eastern: M. carolinensis.
Sheep: Hypopachus cuneus.

**138** Necturus maculosus.
**139** Congo-eel: Amphiuma means.
Hellbender: Cryptobranchus alleghaniensis.
**140** Siren: Siren lacertina.
Mud Siren: Pseudobranchus striatus.
**141** Giant: Dicamptodon ensatus.
Olympic: Rhyacotriton olympicus.
**142** Notophthalmus viridescens viridescens.
**143** Eastern: Notophthalmus viridescens viridescens.
Western: Taricha torosa.
**145** Spotted: Ambystoma maculatum.
Tiger: A. tigrinum.
Marbled: A. opacum.
Jefferson: A. jeffersonianum.
Texas: A. texanum.
**146** Common: Desmognathus fuscus.
Allegheny: D. ochrophaeus.
**147** Red-backed: Plethodon cinereus cinereus.
Slimy: P. glutinosus.
**148** Painted: a. Ensatina eschscholtzi eschscholtzi.
b. E. eschscholtzi klauberi.
Worm: Batrachoseps attenuatus.
**149** Tree: Aneides lugubris.
Green: A. aeneus.
**150** Ozark: Typhlotriton spelaeus.
Texas: Typhlomolge rathbuni.
**151** Red: Pseudotriton ruber.
Purple: Gyrinophilus porphyriticus.
**152** Two-lined: Eurycea bislineata.
Long-tailed: E. longicauda.
Cave: E. lucifuga.
**153** Hemidactylium scutatum.

An asterisk (*) designates pages that are illustrated; **bold type** denotes pages containing more extensive information.

MEASURING SCALE (IN 10THS OF AN INCH)